MAKING RENT

MAKING RENT

The Story Behind the Music that Changed Broadway

TIM WEIL

APOLLO
PUBLISHERS

Making Rent: The Story Behind the Music that Changed Broadway
© 2026 by Tim Weil

All rights reserved. No part of this book may be used or reproduced in any manner whatsoever without the written permission of the publisher, except in the case of brief excerpts in critical reviews or articles. All inquiries should be sent by email to Apollo Publishers at info@apollopublishers.com. Apollo Publishers books may be purchased for educational, business, or sales promotional use. Special editions may be made available upon request. For details, contact Apollo Publishers at info@apollopublishers.com.

Visit our website at www.apollopublishers.com.

Library of Congress Control Number: 2025930935

Print ISBN: 978-1-954641-48-8
Ebook ISBN: 978-1-954641-49-5

Printed in the United States of America.

For more information on Marfan syndrome, please visit the website of the Marfan Foundation at www.marfan.org.

For Al, Nan, Julie, and the boys.

CONTENTS

TUNE UP A BY NEIL PATRICK HARRIS 3
TUNE UP B BY JENNIFER ASHLEY TEPPER 7
NOTE FROM THE AUTHOR 11
INTRO 13
1. DOWNTOWN 17
2. NEXT STEPS 51
3. REHEARSAL 83
4. SUNDAY–MIDWEEK 115
5. NOW WHAT? 123
6. THE TRANSITION 153
7. LIFTOFF 173
8. STEVIE WONDER 187
9. RUNNING 199
OUTRO 243
ACKNOWLEDGMENTS 245
PHOTO CREDITS 247

A billboard in the Hollywood Hills for Rent's *Los Angeles premiere, 1998.*

TUNE UP A
By Neil Patrick Harris

IT'S HIS BOPPING HEAD THAT GOT ME THROUGH IT.
The year was 1997. I was pacing the narrow, claustrophobic lobby hallway of the Coast Playhouse in West Hollywood, clutching fifteen pages of sheet music while trying to simultaneously breathe calmly and appear edgy. I was failing at both. The West Coast production of the juggernaut, zeitgeist-changing musical *Rent* was holding auditions for its principal cast, and I was up next, vying to be narrator/filmmaker/badass Mark Cohen. It was a big swing for me: I'd spent years working in Hollywood, on multiple television series and a few films, but longed to perform onstage in front of an actual audience, in something of substance, with purpose, with heat. I wanted to matter. And *Rent* mattered. It was an extraordinary piece of theater brilliance: current, vibrant, dense, hilarious, gut-wrenching, sexy. It mattered to millions of people, to an entire generation, and it very much mattered to me. This audition could very well alter the course of my life. No pressure.

My name was called. I opened my bottle of water, took one more gulp to quench my frightened, quickly drying mouth, and walked into the theater. I stepped onstage, and there, sitting in the middle of an empty row of theater seats, was one of the original creators of *Rent*, none other than Michael Greif! The brilliant director who had been lockstep with Jonathan Larson himself and molded the raw material into undeniable glory was staring at me through thick glasses and tousled hair, judging my every movement. I tried to act cool but was starting to tremble. To Michael's left was Bernie Telsey, the casting director who had made stars of so many, whose power was palpable. My vocal chords shriveled. Oh god, who else was here? Near the back of the theater was some regular-seeming guy named Tim. Not sure; must have been a producer? I was getting woozy. They asked what I had prepared to sing, and I lumbered to the piano, handing my crumbled pages of sheet music to the accompanist. "'Captain Jack,' by Billy Joel," I stated with confidence, while inside thinking, *Billy Joel?? This is* Rent! *Why didn't you choose Nirvana? Or Bowie? Something cool, but Billy fucking Joel? You're a fraud!* I turned to face them, took one more sip of water, and then the open bottle slipped out of my sweating palms and exploded on the floor, soaking everything around me. Man, I was killing it. And by *it*, I clearly mean my chances.

Before I could hyperventilate or slit a wrist, a voice called out, "'Captain Jack.' I love that song." It came from that nice dude Tim in the back. He was smiling at me with kind eyes. "Great choice; let's go for it." He seemed so calm, so self-assured. His ease reassured me. I took a breath and started to sing. Now, musical theater auditions are typically more theatrical, performative, jazz-handy. I was ill-prepared for being cool, rock and roll, in the pocket. So I started to sing and quickly realized I had no idea what to do with my body. I was just standing there, rigid. I was singing lyrics about tie-dye jeans and masturbating, and just sadly tapping my hand against a thigh. What was I thinking? Why was I thinking? I couldn't get out of my head.

And then I locked eyes with this Tim. He was leaning forward in his seat, attentive, locked in, and bopping his head. No judgment, just moving to the beat. This simple gesture freed me. His head bopping made me feel like I was moving him (which I suppose I literally was, but you know what I mean), like I was being heard (which, again, I literally was, but you know what I . . . ugh, similes are complicated). His head bopping got my head bopping, I became a tad more confident, got out of my own way, and finished "Captain Jack" with a genuine smile. And that moment kind of changed my life.

As I'm sure you have guessed, the aforementioned Tim wasn't some random producer. He was Tim Weil, *Rent*'s OG music supervisor and author of this book. And his act of kindness toward me wasn't singular; it's just who he is and how he lives. You'll soon find out what I mean. I've been lucky enough to work with him twice—once as an actor (I booked the *Rent* gig!) and again as a director (*Rent* at the Hollywood Bowl), and I couldn't have been more appreciative both times. He's a musical genius, an effective collaborator, and an infectious spirit. When you read what's ahead, I think you'll have a greater understanding of why.

Thank you, Tim. For being the coolest guy in the room, for treating others as equals, and for bopping your head to my song. It means more than you know.

rent[1] (rent) *n.* **1a.** Payment, usually of an amount fixed by contract, made by a tenant at specified intervals in return for the right to occupy or use the property of another. **b.** a similar payment made for the use of a facility, equiptment, or service provided by another. **2.** The return derived from cultivated or improved land after deduction of all production costs. **3.** The revenue yielded by a piece of land in excess of that yielded by the poorest of least favorably located land under equal market conditions. In this sense, also called *economic rent.* --**rent** *v.* **rent-ed, rent-ing, rents.** *-tr.* **1.** To obtain occupancy or use of (another's property) in return for regular payments. **2.** To grant temporary occupancy or use of (one's own property or a service) in return for regular payments: *rents out TV sets. -intr.* To be for rent: *The cottage rents for $200 a month. -idiom.* **for rent.** Available for use or service in return for regular payment. (Middle English *rente,* from Old French, from Vulgar Latin **rendita,* from feminine past participle of **rendere,* to yield, return. See RENDER) -**rent'a-bil'-i-ty** *n.* **rent'a-ble** *adj.*

rent[2] (rent) *v.* A past tense and a past participle of **rend.** -**rent** *n.* **1.** An opening made in; a rip. **2.** A breach of relations betweem persons or groups; a rift.

rend (rend) *v.* **rent** (rent) or **rend-ed, rend-ing, rends.** *-tr.* **1.** To tear or split apart or into pieces violently. See Synonyms at **tear**[1] **2.** To tear (one's garments or hair) in anguish or rage. **3.** To tear away forcibly; wrest. **4.** To pull, split, or divide as if by tearing: *"Chip was rent between the impulse to laugh wildly and a bitterness that threatened hot tears"* (Louis Auchincloss). **5.** To pierce or disturb with sound: *a scream rent the silence.* **6.** To cause pain or distress to: *tales that rend the heart. -intr.* To become torn or split: come apart (Middle English, *renden,* from Old English, *rendan*)

A page from Jonathan's notes for Rent.

TUNE UP B
By Jennifer Ashley Tepper

HOW MANY PEOPLE HAVE A FRONT ROW SEAT, to a moment that revolutionizes an entire art form? How many people are an integral part of a musical that breaks significant new ground?

As a theater historian I can tell you that the answer to both of those questions is: Not many. And yet Tim Weil falls into both categories. As the musical director, conductor, keyboard player, co-arranger, and ultimately music supervisor of *Rent*, Weil was right in the thick of the action, contributing profoundly to a major show that transformed the way Broadway sounds today.

Jonathan Larson, who wrote the book, music, and lyrics for *Rent*, spent his whole life dreaming of revolutionizing musical theater—and ultimately he did. Tragically this happened only after Larson's unexpected death at the age of thirty-five, on the night before *Rent* was set to have its first public preview off-Broadway. This cruel timing gave *Rent*'s explosion onto the New York theater scene another layer of meaning. The show's "no day but today" ethos was all the more heartbreaking and resonant.

Broadway in the 1980s and early 1990s was dominated by British imports like *Les Misérables* and *The Phantom of the Opera*.

The decline of Times Square and the loss of countless artists and arts supporters to the AIDS crisis affected the art form and the industry deeply. There were Tony Awards seasons where categories had to be eliminated; the all-important Best Musical category often contained shows that had already closed or revues without original scores. Many Broadway theaters sat empty. The golden age of Broadway was long gone.

Then *Rent* happened.

The brilliant musical was a landmark success that introduced a new generation to the theater. It ushered in the contemporary era of rock and pop musicals on Broadway. It brought ticket accessibility to Broadway via rush and lottery systems. It fought for social and political messages to be heard onstage, included a diverse array of characters, and showed theater makers what musicals at their best could be. Musical theater is one of the great American art forms, and *Rent* reclaimed it, inspiring a worldwide revitalization.

Rent was first born when Jonathan Larson was connected with the playwright Billy Aronson by developer of new musicals Ira Weitzman. Aronson had had the idea to adapt Giacomo Puccini's nineteenth century opera *La bohème* into a musical and was looking for a composer. Though Larson and Aronson briefly collaborated, Aronson departed the project after they'd crafted three songs together, giving Larson his blessing to keep developing it. Larson, for his part, was deeply moved by the notion of bringing the opera's characters to his own contemporary New York City. While *Rent* was not autobiographical, the opera's characters, who live in poverty and sacrifice everything for their art and ideals, had much in common with Larson's eclectic group of downtown artist friends. Rodolfo the poet and Marcello the painter became Roger the rock musician and Mark the filmmaker, familiar figures in the East Village of the 1980s. Seeing a connection between the deadly tuberculosis that affects the opera's characters and the HIV/AIDS epidemic that had already claimed several of Larson's close friends, he developed several characters in ways that would prove groundbreaking. Mimi, who in the opera is a seamstress living with tuberculosis, became an S-M dancer addicted to heroin and living with AIDS. Multiple queer couples, also grappling with the scourge of the epidemic, were included in the main cast. In adjusting *La bohème*'s character map so that *Rent* could explore women who love women and men who love men, Larson made the visibility of the LGBTQ+ community a priority. While a plethora of plot points, story elements, and character traits have parallels in *La bohème*, *Rent* is very much an original musical, a postmodern take on *La bohème* rather than a literal adaptation.

Just as *La bohème* shook the opera world when it opened in Italy in 1896, *Rent* had a massive effect when it opened on Broadway exactly a century later. *Rent*'s impact can't be overstated, and the nearly sung-through musical's brilliant score was an essential key to its triumph. If you're reading these words, I guarantee you have sung along to "Seasons of Love" or "La Vie Boheme." The songs in *Rent* struck a deep chord with millions, but while Larson's contributions to the American theater have been covered profusely, Weil's contributions to *Rent*'s musical success, through his collaboration with Larson and his completion of the score after Larson's death, have not been covered in any meaningful detail.

Making Rent is a window into the process of creating a new musical from the perspective of the head of the music department. It's a perspective that has rarely been told. Music supervisors and musical directors are absolutely essential to musicals, and yet we almost never hear the story from their point of view. Any documentation of the creation of *Rent* from a team member is valuable, and to hear from the man who was at the keys from the very beginning is uniquely compelling. Weil was leading the band, giving creative input about the score, and mourning his friend and collaborator as *Rent* catapulted into the stratosphere. He takes us into the scrappy atmosphere of New York Theatre Workshop in the mid-1990s, developing *Rent*. We sit with him and Larson at auditions for now-iconic actors from the original cast. We keep him company as he navigates unprecedented success. Weil's insight was invaluable to me when I was putting together the off-Broadway musical *The Jonathan Larson Project*, and for future scholars, musical directors, and theater makers, this vital text will surely inform the way *Rent* is thought about for years to come.

NOTE FROM THE AUTHOR

Making Rent is my account of how we ushered *Rent* from a small theater in New York's East Village to Broadway and then the world. For the most part I relied on my own memories, notes, music, and journals, as well as materials on file in the Jonathan Larson Papers at the Library of Congress, some of which was material I donated from my years with the show. I also conducted interviews with all the book's major players to verify certain information. Those interviews helped me to construct my narrative, and the discoveries of where our recollections intersected confirmed and, much to my great joy, unlocked more memories than I anticipated. When you come across quotes from some of those people, they have been directly lifted from our interviews. Julie Larson, Jonathan's sister, as well as a handful of Jonathan's closest friends—Jonathan Burkhart, Victoria Leacock Hoffman, Matt O'Grady, and Todd Robinson—were very generous with their time and shared memories and photos you'll find throughout.

Jonathan on his thirty-fifth birthday at The Bowery Bar, New York City. February 4, 1995.

INTRO

ON THE MORNING OF JANUARY 25, 1996, I was getting myself together to head downtown early for what I thought would be a normal day of rehearsal. The night before we had completed our final run-through of Jonathan Larson's new musical, *Rent*, but there was still some work to be done before our first preview for a paying audience that night. I wanted to get a jump start on the day. But around 7:30 Sue White, the production manager at the New York Theatre Workshop, called. She asked if I was sitting down and then broke the news. Jonathan had died early that morning, sometime between 1:00 and 3:30 a.m., not long after he and I had parted ways.

Jonathan and I had been working together since the fall of 1994, when I was brought onto the *Rent* team, first as an audition pianist and then as the show's musical director. That was the same year that Michael Greif joined as director. At the time *Rent* was little more than a blip on the downtown theater landscape, and there was no reason for any of us to expect that it would go on to permeate the performing arts world the way it would. Certainly on that frigid January morning, the idea of our show having an impact on anyone besides us—the cast, the creative team, and the Workshop—was unimaginable.

Of course, in the months to follow, *Rent* would tear through America's popular culture with a force few Broadway musicals have matched since. Besides its obvious influence on the composers, lyricists, and librettists who have created musical theater in its wake, its characters, song titles, a random lyric from "La Vie Boheme," and even some of the actors' real names started routinely showing up in daily crossword puzzles around the country. Never in a million years would I have imagined our show, from its humble beginnings, burrowing that deeply into the national lexicon.

Others have written and will write about *Rent* as a piece of theater, a pop culture phenomenon, and about its place in the history of the theater. As I see it though, what's most noteworthy about *Rent*, its greatest achievement and the thing that will continue to shape musical theater well into the future, is its music. Jonathan's fierce determination to bring the contemporary popular music he grew up with into the theater will resonate for decades to come. In the months leading up to his death, he had written ferociously. Some of his best-known songs had been completed in the last weeks of his life. Together he and I, along with the *Rent* band, had taken his songs and fleshed them out into completely orchestrated numbers—dropping notes here, adding chords there, and developing his score to a level that, much to our own surprise, would become iconic. So much of our work was finished by January 25, 1996, but there was still more to do. That's how theater is made. Now that he was gone, we would have to carry on the work we had assumed he would be there to finish with us. Where we once had Jonathan to give us clear answers to our questions, we would now only have our experience, artistry, and each other to rely upon.

The police had apparently called Sue, as the Workshop's point of contact, well before sunup to explain what happened and what they knew. Jonathan had died of an aortic aneurysm that ruptured. *Burst, blew up, exploded. Pick your verbiage,* I thought. *Doesn't matter.* If there was the slightest bit of comfort to be taken, the police told Sue, it was that Jonathan was dead before he hit the floor. *No, no comfort in that.*

Montauk, New York. I should have taken that gig. You know, free clams.

DOWNTOWN
1994

"HELLO?"

"Hi. Is this Tim?"

"Yeah, hi. Who's this?"

"My name is Martha Banta. I'm with the New York Theatre Workshop. We're a nonprofit theater in the East Village and we're looking for an audition pianist for a rock opera we're doing this fall," she said, before adding, "The pay's not so great. It's only ten dollars an hour. Is there any chance you'd be available?"

That's how it started. Unremarkably. I needed the money, even ten dollars an hour, but I was also intrigued. I had been subbing on Broadway for *The Who's Tommy* off and on, and I remember asking myself, *Who's writing a rock opera nowadays?* And while the pay was light, it would only be a short gig, and a rock opera was in my wheelhouse. The altruist in me put in his two cents too, suggesting that it would be nice to help a nonprofit get its show going, even in a small way. So after Martha gave me the dates and times, off I went. Subsequently, I found out that she had called six other people before me (her list was alphabetical), and I was the only one who said yes, either because the previous six weren't home, didn't return her call, or, more likely, wouldn't play auditions for ten dollars an hour. I, however, was becoming more desperate by the week.

I had arrived in New York City in 1982, freshly graduated from the New England Conservatory of Music in Boston, with the goal of becoming a freelance musician and musical director, and what money I had, all of it, was gone after I paid my first and last month's rent plus a security deposit. I was in New York barely five hours and already I was flat broke.

I explored the city by taking the subway to different neighborhoods and walking around. One day I was strolling up Eighth Avenue and came upon a sign in a window between Twenty-Eighth and Twenty-Ninth Streets: "Wanted. Piano player—two nights a week for cabaret series." I must have had a trustworthy face, because they hired me without an audition. I didn't know anything about the music or the gig. All I knew was that it paid sixty dollars cash for one hour, twice a week. The first night I played for an Edith Piaf imitator followed by a stripper/folk singer. She wore a G-string and had an acoustic guitar strapped around her body. I played two songs with each of them, collected my sixty dollars, and said see you later. I left feeling all the more confident I was in the right city.

Over time my career formed along two paths, theatrical and musical. A reading here (my first one was titled *Theda Bara and the Frontier Rabbi*), a blues band there, an off-off-Broadway show here, a bus-and-truck tour there. For a few years during the mid-eighties I was the musical director of the revival of *Oh! Calcutta!* on Broadway. I didn't get paid Broadway money because it was a "special" contract, but I made a nice living for a few years. The show was a relic of the late sixties, an erotic counterculture revue with full nudity in some places, but thankfully not in the band. Doing that show was my first encounter with the golden handcuffs. It was a great steady gig and a great living, but not at all what I wanted out of the theater, and at a certain point I had to leave, money be damned. I was broke before, and if I was going to be broke again, so be it. I was becoming a better musician, and

MAKING RENT
(19)

I was confident that my career would head toward a better place. I had to close that door so another one might open. Back to freelancing I went.

I booked cabaret gigs, singer-songwriter gigs, and club dates, which was code for weddings. Club dates were, more often than not, uniquely soul-sucking gigs. They paid well and I learned a lot of repertoire, but playing weddings could be professionally abusive. While we all knew that the music we played—from light classical to Motown—was still art, the people we were working for didn't necessarily have that front of mind. They just wanted to celebrate the occasion—get married, eat, drink, and dance. The trouble with that was that somewhere in that equation the musicians became slightly dehumanized. Yes, we knew that we were working in service to the occasion, but in that blur of celebration came the inevitable, alcohol-soaked, the-band-is-our-bitch attitude that was transmitted, not so subtly, from the hirers to the hired. For seemingly endless weekends the gigs felt like "bus this table," "play that tune," "bring out the main course," "play something we can all dance to," "sweep the carpet," "play a hora," and I started to realize that playing live music on those gigs existed on the same plane as mopping up spilled champagne. Eventually I was lucky enough to hook up with a regular group, the Rhythm Dogs, which made the club dates and better-paying corporate gigs significantly more tolerable. Apart from that world there was a South American tour of the musical *Blues in the Night*, a concert tour with a cheesy French pop star, and, eventually, subbing on Broadway shows.

Those early Broadway subbing experiences gave me a lot of insight into the level of accomplishment and musicianship I needed to bring to the epicenter of musical theater, which in turn provided me with a humbling kick in the ass. Starting in the 1960s and continuing through the 1970s, a lot of the traditional money-making gigs for working musicians, like recording sessions or commercial jingles, started drying up. When we hit the 1980s and the digital domain started to rule, sound libraries and affordable highly adaptable recording studios (called project studios) became the new normal and put a lot of musicians out of business. So Broadway shows, still played by live musicians, quickly became among the better-paying regular gigs. The result was that they started attracting a much higher caliber of musician. The level of musicianship—and therefore competition—from the 1980s on grew exponentially.

In the beginning I just wasn't good enough. I'd practice the book (the music) at home, and then I'd be allowed to practice on the keyboard setup in the theater at designated times. After I did a show once or twice, I was either officially approved by the conductor or not. At first I had my share of not. After a time I learned to prepare better and I became more proficient at showing up and not screwing up, which resulted in more shows and an improving reputation.

By the early nineties I was rolling along pretty nicely, and since I had acquired a volume of musical theater experience under my belt, I also started doing some private coaching. But then, out of the blue, I went from plenty busy to almost nothing in short order. This wasn't exactly new to me—in college I had certainly had the experience of gigs being canceled last minute or steady work drying up suddenly. But this was my first financial body blow as a young professional without the foundation of the conservatory and all the support it provided. That's sometimes what happens when you're a young freelancer, I reminded myself; nothing is promised or steady, and the field is crowded and competitive. Which is all to say that I needed the ten bucks an hour the New York Theatre Workshop was offering. I knew little about the Workshop, or NYTW, from my time in the New York theater world but would come to learn that it had been founded in 1979 by Stephen Graham and was initially known as the Stephen

MAKING RENT

Graham Foundation. Its mission was to support writers and directors specifically. In 1983 it was reincorporated as the New York Theatre Workshop and in 1988 Jim Nicola was tapped to be its artistic director. Jim's approach was in line Stephen's original vision but he put his own spin on the Workshop's artistic direction. Rather than set up a competitive environment, he aspired to connect the theater community to itself, identifying writers, designers, and directors, all with the intent of prioritizing art as much as commerce. In New York's cutthroat, fiercely competitive theater scene, Jim sought to bring creative people together instead of pitting them against each other. He would mount productions and invite the creators' peers to collaborate, constructively critique, and support the work. The spirit of that approach was ultimately what set NYTW apart from many of the other theater institutions south of Fourteenth Street.

As the Workshop's operations expanded under Jim's leadership, its staff sought a home base from which they could better execute their vision, and in 1992 they moved to a fledgling theater at 79 East Fourth Street. Once a garage and repair warehouse for the city's garbage trucks, the space had been transformed into a 150-seat venue, originally known as the Truck and Warehouse Theater.

The same year the Workshop moved to its permanent location, a young composer–lyricist named Jonathan Larson rode his bicycle across East Fourth Street with a libretto and a demo tape in his knapsack. He stopped in front of the New York Theatre Workshop. Coincidentally, the production manager at the time, George Xenos, was out in front of the theater. Jonathan got off his bicycle, introduced himself, gave George the material, and said, "This is where I want to do my musical." George passed that material on to Jim, who read the libretto and listened to the demo tape that came with it. He was immediately struck by how the work seemed to be a celebration of the East Village and its residents. *What an incredible way to celebrate the Workshop's new home*, he thought. Despite the overwhelming prospect of staging an ambitious and lengthy rock opera with a twelve-person cast, to Jim this work by a songwriter with an original, theatrical, and inspiring voice had great possibilities, and that's what NYTW was about: possibilities.

On my first commute to NYTW I headed down by way of two subway trains and a half-mile walk from Astor Place to East Fourth Street. I had spent a lot of time in the East Village during my halcyon rock and roll years, my mid-twenties into my early thirties. I had been in some bands, a couple of which, we'd been told, were on the verge of getting record deals. It was what record companies told everyone, but it gave us hope and incentive. I played at CBGB a handful of times, a few of them showcasing for labels, with pretty good rock bands, but wasn't part of anything groundbreaking or all that original. So no record deal ever materialized.

Had I taken a slightly different route to the Workshop, as I would in nicer weather, I would have taken a combination of the 1, 2, or 3 trains and gotten off at Christopher Street in the West Village. On my walk east to the Workshop I would have passed a whole slew of clubs I had played in the eighties and early nineties, on Bleecker Street and in the surrounding neighborhoods: Cafe Wha?, The Bitter End, Kenny's Castaways, and Village Gate, continuing eastward to the Milk Bar (a short-lived 1980s rock club with a killer sound system), Peppermint Lounge, Tramps, and a few others that were home to many musicians like me and bands like the ones I was playing in: rock and roll's vast middle class.

In those years the farther east you walked, the more menacing the surroundings became. Alphabet City even came with its own adage: If you walked down Avenue A, you were all right; Avenue B, you were brave; Avenue C, you were crazy; and Avenue D, you were dead. There were lots of junkies and dealers on stoops of apartment buildings, broken glass and empty crack vials strewn about, and homeless people everywhere. I had played at a couple of the well-known Avenue A spots like the Pyramid Club (a drag mecca where RuPaul and Lady Bunny performed), Brownies, and the Mercury Lounge, as well as a few other no-signage nightspots. As dangerous as the neighborhood seemed at the time, I kind of felt I belonged there. *This is who I am*, I thought. I was a theater and rock guy, working in clubs all over Manhattan, so the walk down Avenue A or B wasn't uncomfortable for me. Also I used to buy drugs on the streets in those neighborhoods, which made the surroundings oddly hospitable, especially since the bands I was with were repeat customers. I didn't venture eastward of Avenue B for obvious reasons, but no matter the neighborhood, once I got inside those clubs, all I felt was pride in their history and an eagerness for the gig.

On my first day at NYTW, I walked into that very groovy theater and made my way down the aisle to the piano. The theater felt welcoming and like cool, informed work happened there. The crew that had assembled was friendly as well. Those were the people who formed the creative foundation of *Rent*: Michael Greif, Jim Nicola; casting director Wendy Ettinger; Martha Banta, who had called me about the job; and the musical director. It was very kind of everyone to stand up, greet me, and shake my hand. From my midtown audition pianist experiences, I had rarely, if ever, been greeted so warmly. I appreciated their easy politeness and decency, considering I was just there to do a job for a few days. The last person to stand up and greet me unfolded himself from his theater seat. He was tall and lanky, all shoulders, elbows, and knees, with big hands and long, skinny fingers. Piano players take note of hands like those. His face was framed by hair that had been cut short on the sides and in the back but left a mess of curls on top, which made him look even taller. I imagined that in his younger days it would have been a white man's Afro, or as I had called it in my Jewish youth, an Isro. He said, "Hi, I'm Jonathan." I would find out soon that he was the musical's composer and lyricist. Before I got to the piano, I saw him fold himself back into his seat. The whole folding-and-unfolding thing had a real origami vibe to it.

A normal audition day in musical theater would go like this: The singer would have rehearsed and memorized his or her material prior to the audition, then brought in the sheet music so the pianist could accompany them. The music would have been prepared and marked appropriately so the pianist could easily follow, and the auditions would be fairly seamless. What I experienced during the first days of *Rent* auditions bore little resemblance to that process. The people who came in for the auditions at the Workshop that first day were, to put it mildly, all over the yard. Some had brought handwritten music, just numbers and letters scrawled on notebook paper and folded—or in a couple instances balled up. Some came with lyrics and no music, some came with music and no lyrics, some came only with chords, and not necessarily in the right key. In a few cases, the music and singing were so disconnected from each other that I just stopped playing and let the person sing a cappella. No harm, no foul. The truth was, many of those performers didn't know how to prepare music, much less prepare for a musical theater audition. I was game for all that. As a college student I had spent a few summers music directing shows at a fine arts camp for girls and young women where, aside from being introduced to the genius of Stephen Sondheim, I learned that what I loved about working in the theater was teaching performers the music they would be singing. A part of that teaching is caretaking, and I was a natural at both.

And so here at the *Rent* auditions my caretaking instinct kicked in, and after the first few performers I realized that my job was to help the singers get through their auditions as best I could, come what may. For instance, when someone didn't have music with them, I asked what songs they knew, even if it was just a part of a song. The easiest go-to option was "Happy Birthday," and I tried to accommodate by playing it in many keys. The fact that the audition was for a rock opera meant that the most appropriate material was rock, pop, or R & B, which to the performers' credit was what many of them brought in, despite how unorganized or incorrect their sheet music might have been. And I was familiar with most of that style of material: I could easily handle nearly anything by R.E.M., The Police, Aretha Franklin, and Peter Gabriel—even artists as diverse as Nirvana, Stevie Wonder, Elvis Costello, and Prince, and in some cases, more pop-rock theater stuff, like songs from *Les Misérables, The Who's Tommy,* and *Hair,* with maybe a dash of *Pippin.*

Throughout the day performers came in, sang, maybe chatted with the creatives for a bit, and left. After each had gone, there would be a little conversation about the person's performance. That early part of the process was where the initial collaboration of director, composer-lyricist, and musical director began to take shape, as they figured out their tastes and their own group dynamics in real time. Who likes whom, why or why not, and whether they should call the performer back are all part of the getting-to-know-you process for any creative team. It took about half of the morning session to catch wind of the beginnings of a tension in the room. Michael and the musical director had radically different taste and takes on the performers, leaving Jonathan stuck in the middle. He had hired the musical director without Michael's approval, and the early part of the collaboration clearly wasn't going well.

As the auditions continued, and as I kept doing my audition pianist thing, I noticed that the musical director never chimed in to do any music directing. I continued to do my best trying to help every performer present himself or herself in their best way musically. Maybe Michael and Jonathan noticed, because after lunch, during the afternoon session, they started asking my opinion about the auditions. "Tim, do you think they could sing that note?" "What do you think about their vocal stamina?"

They asked me things that the musical director wasn't able, or willing, to answer. I limited my responses to as few words as possible because I was only the audition pianist, and in the traditional pecking order an audition pianist didn't typically give an opinion. Also I had a history with the musical director—including having just worked under him at another off-Broadway show prior to those auditions—so I didn't want to disrespect him. In retrospect I'm sure that's how NYTW got my name. They probably asked Jonathan if he knew any pianists who might work for low pay, and Jonathan, in turn, asked his musical director if he knew anyone.

What I remember most about that first day is that I had never played auditions for such a diverse group of performers. I accompanied men, women, some androgynous folks that the farm boy in me couldn't quite figure out, Black, Latin, white, Asian, young, old, in between, the whole deal. Also members of what was then simply referred to as the gay community (the LBGTQ+ acronym was still years away). I felt like I played for everyone who wanted to be heard. The day went off as advertised, truly an open call. It was happily the most unique theater experience I had ever been involved in up to that point in my career.

The auditioners were also diverse in accomplishment, preparedness, and skill. From my perspective there were around four or five auditions that stood out during those first days. The first was from early on day one when Anthony Rapp came in. He was young, charming, a little quirky, and as we all soon found out, smart and talented. He put R.E.M.'s "Losing My Religion" in front of me and then sang it well, with near-perfect pitch and great rhythm and clarity. His sound had a great print, my own personal measurement of a singing voice with a unique and appealing identity. After he left the theater, Jonathan exclaimed, "That's Mark!" No one argued. I guess they found what they were looking for. They knew the character. Easy. Done. One down, eleven to go.

Sometime that day or the next, a friend of Martha's named Gilles Chiasson came in. Gilles had been on the *Les Misérables* tour for a while, so it wasn't his first audition experience; he was a young pro already. He handed me his music, his own arrangement of Billy Joel's "Goodnight Saigon" set in a slightly higher key than the original, so with that along with the song's triumphant feel it was reminiscent of *Les Mis*. It was clear he'd sung it often. Like Anthony, he had the ability to bend a pop song into a more theatrical rendition, which told me they both were tuned into the acting as well as the singing. He had incredible range, along with a sweet, soaring, mature-beyond-his-years tenor, and he seemed grounded and friendly, a regular guy. To my mind, those traits mattered. Even though he didn't get the definitive thumbs-up from the creatives, I assumed all of them knew that strong, legit tenors at such a young age were a rarity. I felt that if they fit the play, they should be cast. They'd be worth their weight in vocal gold.

On the second day, a beautiful, groovy young woman named Daphne Rubin-Vega came in. She was in a girl group that people knew at the time called Pajama Party, and she brought in "Roxanne" by The Police. Another great choice and a song I knew well. I played the intro, waiting for her to come in, and eventually she did, singing "Roxanne"—but she didn't finish the verse. We got to the top of the second verse and again she sang, "Roxanne," but didn't finish that verse either. We arrived at the pre-chorus and she sang "Roxanne" but didn't sing the lyric, which should have been "You don't have to put on the red light." Basically all Daphne sang was "Roxanne," top to bottom. It was kind of hilarious.

She knew where all the lyrics were in the tune, but for whatever reason, she didn't sing them. So I started to sing a little from the piano to give her some support, hoping she would start singing everything in between the Roxannes. But it was to no avail. She was just unprepared, guileless, and in a completely unfamiliar environment. The easy guess for everyone was that the theater wasn't her world. Amazingly, she seemed unfazed by it all, maybe a bit off-balance, but resilient. Even from my standpoint, as I tried to help her give a proper audition, I was charmed; her presence, aura, and spirit were rare and appealing.

The creatives went nuts over her. Everyone *loved* her. Well, almost everyone. While no one had the opportunity to hear her sing the song straight through, I think the creatives heard enough to be encouraged by her audition. She sang high enough, I guessed, though I didn't know the vocal range of the character she auditioned for. And like Anthony Rapp's a day earlier, her voice had a great print. Even I knew she was one of one. And yet Jonathan wasn't sold. He had a certain voice in his mind and Daphne wasn't it, at least not at that point. Later, Wendy Ettinger would call her and say that the creative team really liked her and wanted to bring her back, but she had to come in fully prepared. They gave her a song from the show called "Valentine's Day." It was a straight-up rock song that would require range and stamina.

We saw a bunch of great folks on those initial audition days. Among them was Shelley Dickinson, who had come off John Kander and Fred Ebb's *The World Goes 'Round* and was eventually cast as Joanne. Sarah Knowlton, who was cast as Maureen, brought her cello to the audition and played well. She knew what I didn't, that the character of Maureen was a performance artist and musician in the vein of Laurie Anderson, so her cello playing could be a valuable asset. There was also Tony Hoylen, a great singer with a flourishing voice-over career; Pat Briggs, a solid rocker who could sing multiple notes at once (called multiphonics), which I had only previously heard musicians do while playing an instrument; Michael Potts, a great actor; and Erin Hill, a phenomenal singer and musician.

The days came and went, and with them the same slightly uncomfortable "Tim, what did you think?" It wasn't better or worse than the days before, but the tension among the creative team hung in the air. I felt bad that they were going through that, something I hadn't ever personally experienced, and I figured it was something they would address eventually, but in the moment they had auditions to complete and a show to cast.

After the first round of auditions were over I went home, expecting to put the tension to bed, but later that night my phone rang. It was Jonathan, and as soon as he identified himself, I knew what was coming. He said he wanted to fire the musical director but first wanted to know if I would be interested in music directing the show. I told him I was interested but I would have to work around a few conflicts I couldn't get out of, and I asked if he could give me some time to get back to him. The truth was that I had really enjoyed the audition experience and had liked Michael, Jim, and Jonathan immediately, as well as the feeling of the Workshop. I was rooting for the performers, many of whom were from off the theater farm, and I was hoping they would find a place in Jonathan's musical. I knew I was a great fit, and I knew I could help those who weren't confident singers, and that appealed to me. I wanted to be a part of all that.

I eventually learned all the events that precipitated Jonathan's call. At the auditions, while tension was building behind where I was stationed at the piano, Jonathan was auditioning me. Apparently after the first few days, Michael made it clear to Jonathan that he didn't want to work with the musical director, and Jonathan had no problem with finding someone new. Martha held up my résumé, which I had given her on the first day, and said, "How about Tim?" I would say yes, of course, and ultimately become the musical director of the *Rent* workshop in 1994. It certainly was a plot twist for the seventh person called to be the audition pianist. I didn't believe much in coincidences. I believed in things like stars crossing perfectly in the right space and time, and this felt like the epitome of that.

The next day Jonathan messengered over the score, which was both musically dense and physically heavy. Jonathan had printed out the entire piano-vocal score, which had been entered on a new digital program called ConcertWare that was designed for Macintosh computers. It was just shy of five hundred pages of single-sided, difficult-to-read music (both notes and lyrics). I slogged my way through it, note by note, word by word, penciling in a lot for my own clarity, so I could teach it better and quicker, and strangely I got used to reading the illegible. It was a difficult software program to master and format, and Jonathan had done his best. He certainly couldn't have afforded to have someone else do it.

Between the call from Jonathan and throughout the callbacks, he and I would talk on the phone a bit, getting to know each other. We talked about college, his experience at Adelphi University on Long Island, and mine at the conservatory in Boston. In his free time during his college years, he wrote cabaret shows, and in mine I wrote horn charts for a band my friends and I had formed called Confunkatory, which should tell you everything you need to know about the musical direction we took. As a college student I had gotten deep into the synergy of jazz, pop, and R & B that was exemplified by landmark albums from Joni Mitchell (*Court and Spark*, 1975), Steely Dan (*Aja*, 1977), Herbie Hancock (*Head Hunters*, 1973), and Earth, Wind & Fire (*That's the Way of the World*, 1975). These albums showed me that my jazz and harmonic knowledge could, and should, be applied to songs with a contemporary backbeat and lyrics. By incorporating the Motown-inspired soul and R & B of the 1960s with jazz and funk elements, and backing them with African and Latin percussion, these musicians had pushed pop music into a completely expansive new continuum.

I told Jonathan about my influences and my love for rock, pop, jazz, Latin music, R & B, and gospel. Jonathan wasn't into funk, R & B, and world music the way I was, but we had an overlapping appreciation for Billy Joel and Stephen Sondheim. Jonathan told me that Billy Joel was a big influence on his piano playing, especially as a rock pianist (something not uncommon for suburban white boys in the 1970s), and that Sondheim was his theatrical idol, which was due in part to the cleverness and sophistication of his lyric writing and the multiple ways in which Sondheim's rhyme schemes always surprised and delighted him. That connected with me, given that Sondheim's groundbreaking show *Company* had been my gateway to the musical theater my first summer at the girls camp. The first two chords of *Company*'s opening number could have been in any of the jazz tunes I was learning, and once I heard the rhyming of "personable" with "co-ercin' a bull" in the song "You Could Drive a Person Crazy," I was officially all in.

Understanding those connections clarified much of Jonathan's work for me. I had been going through the score, and his piano style was indeed very much like Billy Joel's, with a little early Stephen Schwartz in there, and it also included some distinctive eighties harmonies that gave Jonathan's work a modern edge— think Bruce Hornsby and Ben Folds. That style paired nicely with the emotional resonance and dramatic structure of his lyrics that, it had become clear to me, had their roots in musical theater. All of this led me to think that for a contemporary theater writer, a postmodern marriage between Billy Joel and Stephen Sondheim seemed like a good foundation on which to build.

Jonathan asked me what I could do as a musician other than play piano and work with singers, and I told him that I could do whatever he needed. I had done a lot of vocal arranging and had composed and orchestrated the music for the Broadway show *Sally Marr . . . and Her Escorts*, starring Joan Rivers, just a few months prior. Whatever he needed musically, I'd be a willing resource—something that, considering that we were a tiny operation, came as good news to him. He could continue developing the show with Michael, writing new songs or composing new music, and I'd be able to take care of nearly anything music-related that he wanted me to take care of.

What connected us most was the possibility that pop and rock could intersect with musical theater in a meaningful way. For me that idea was pretty basic. What had held me back from fully diving into the theater as a young person was that the music didn't groove. I never felt anything physically, only intellectually. And let's be clear: Sondheim's intellect was both lyrically and harmonically on a superior level, like a super-grandmaster in chess. But did the music groove? Absolutely not. The main separator of contemporary pop music from traditional theater music is pop's heavy reliance on a rhythm section—typically guitars, bass, drums, and keyboards. The toolbox for a rhythm section is different from that of an orchestra but just as plentiful. Why not put all the great things about musical theater writing—particularly the depth of emotions the music and lyrics are able to convey—over those grooves, which can be altered to fit what is happening onstage dramatically? Not every groove is a simple *boom! thwack! boom! thwack!* There are infinite rhythmic and stylistic variations, dynamics, tempos, styles, and feels that any rhythm section worth its salt can play, but rock and pop bands are mostly heard under the umbrella of radio-friendly musical traditions, which can generally be characterized by tight musical structures and simple, easy-to-digest lyrics. The vast majority of mainstream pop hits are written within a limited range so people who aren't singers can sing along with them, which is an intentional, calculated play by the music industry. An important, maybe *the* most important, rule about a rock or pop song meant for airplay is this: simple is good, complex isn't. If a song doesn't grab its listener in the first ten seconds, the person will change stations.

In the theater, more complicated song structures, wider vocal ranges, and more nuanced storytelling are huge dramatic assets. It was clear from those early conversations with Jonathan that we'd both contemplated all those possibilities for some time before we met, and we found common purpose in those ideas. After those initial phone calls and the occasional cup of coffee or tea, we knew we were on solid ground together. At the very least we had a complementary musical and theatrical outlook that we could go forward with over the following weeks.

As we got on to the business of what was ahead of us, we had to finish casting the show and hire a band. But what kind of band? That became a thoughtful, thorough conversation between us—typical of Jonathan and his curious mind. Jonathan was way ahead of his time. He had fleshed out some demos of him singing his own material at home to use when he submitted his work to potential producers. He accomplished that using only a couple pieces of early digital keyboard technology and a microphone for his vocals. They conveyed his ideas well, clearly rock and pop influenced, but were limited in what they could produce sonically. Still, I thought he'd used the few devices he owned very creatively to get his songs recorded in his unique, postmodern style. He was original in all areas of his detailed thinking, and eventually he was introduced to a great keyboardist and producer I knew named Steve Skinner. They struck a deal and over time produced fantastic demos in Steve's studio, which was a playground of keyboards, drum machines, early sampling technology, digital recorders, and effects, like reverb and delay. Steve was a great programmer, engineer, and producer, as well as a fine keyboardist in his own right. Together they would create tracks and Jonathan would have people he knew from the theater world, or simply friends who could sing, come in and do those demos with him. Since the finished products sounded great, it made sense in Jonathan's forward-thinking mind that it would be cool if the band consisted of four keyboard players and a drummer, because that's how his best demos were generated.

I took the counterargument. The equipment Steve had in his studio was high-end and costly. I had some gear, but nothing close to the quality of what Steve had. Neither did Jonathan. To ask four keyboard players to get equipment like that, whether renting or buying it, or even ask the Workshop to rent or buy all the gear we'd need wasn't possible—they wouldn't be able or willing to make that kind of financial commitment to the show. I certainly couldn't afford it, so I couldn't ask others to pony up. And even if we somehow had the equipment, we would be working under Michael and Jonathan's desire to have the band onstage, so we'd never be able to re-create what Steve had done in a studio setting. Steve was a genius at what he did, and live digital performance hadn't reached that level of excellence yet. For instance, digital keyboards at the time could never have come close to replicating the sound of an electric guitar and the effects they could produce using the analog pedals that had then been around for a few decades. I was certain the results wouldn't simply be disappointing for Jonathan and his audiences; they would sound cold, unnatural, and sterile.

My pitch to Jonathan was to use a rock band as the musical canvas for his songs, and if we could play grunge versions of some of his songs, all the better. I felt that approach lent itself well to his sound, and bands like Nirvana, Pearl Jam, Alice in Chains, and the Smashing Pumpkins were popular at that time, so the music would sound current and recognizable, particularly among the younger theater-going audiences Jonathan wanted his show to target. The classic rock band with a modern approach would be a good end point because it would leave plenty of room for Jonathan's Billy Joel–influenced piano playing, which was the centerpiece of a lot of his musical vocabulary. And I knew it was a better fit dramatically to have a band onstage that resembled what was happening in the clubs and on the streets of the East Village. Michael and I never spoke about it, but maybe we didn't have to. Had Jonathan been determined to go with the keyboards and four computer terminals, or any other way, I would have made do, but he was cool with what I proposed. That was the beginning of our collaboration—born out of logic and necessity, with our musical tastes intersecting.

The start of callbacks meant that we were going to see Daphne again. She'd been tasked with preparing a song from the show we'd given her time with, and man, was she ready this time. She nailed the audition. She'd memorized the song and she sang great. She even made some acting choices, which told everyone that she had thought about the lyrics and what they meant to her version of the character Mimi. She brought everything Michael, Jim, and I expected out of a callback. Even with a clear ask, success hadn't been a given: this was still a new world to her. But she showed up and she showed her vocal skill, artistry, and smarts all in a span of three minutes. I knew even then that her first audition experience had been a real teaching moment. When the casting director tells you the creative team likes you, you go home, learn your material, kill it, and make that casting decision easy for them.

We cast her, though Jonathan still had some trepidation about her singing, specifically around her stamina. Daphne didn't have a traditional musical theater singer's voice; it was more reedy. It was her own unique sound, and I saw and heard what Jonathan didn't. Technically speaking, her breathing was well supported, from her diaphragm, and she knew the full capacity of her voice. She sang *smart*. I heard that in both of her auditions. Still, she had a lot to sing in his show and he asked me directly if I thought she'd hold up. She was small in stature and her voice was nontraditional, so it was a legitimate question that he had every right to ask. But I was confident she could handle the role vocally. I had been through the score a handful of times by then and understood the challenge that would need to be met, and I was more than comfortable sticking my neck out for Daphne, and I told him so.

"Yeah, she will. And if she needs help, I can help her," I said.

Of course she needed very little of my help, but happily Daphne was safe. I wish I could say we gave her the confidence and long-term security we had given Anthony and Gilles, but for the moment it would have to be enough. Some days later *Rent* was fully cast and ready to roll. We had a three-week rehearsal process with the cast and eventually folded in the four-piece rock band before our six public performances over a ten-day period. All this from early October to mid-November 1994.

Rehearsal began with a song Jonathan had written called "Seasons of Love." He had written it a couple of years earlier as a response to a playful challenge from his girlfriend, who had told him he couldn't write a gospel song. Not only did he succeed in meeting that challenge, it became the centerpiece of the show's ethos while miraculously fitting into Jonathan's harmonic world that the show inhabited. It was the opening to act two, and Michael thought it would be a great place to start music rehearsal. As I would come to learn, his instincts were dead-on. Jonathan had recorded the song at home a couple years earlier, and he gave me his demo to check out. Between the recording and a poorly executed musical printout, I came into rehearsal with some thoughts and questions about the vocals, but I wasn't sure if it was my place to raise them. Even though I knew it was only a home demo, I didn't think the song was fully realized. The melody, the piano part, and the lyrics struck me as being beyond ridiculous. Jonathan had found the alchemy of his songwriter's taste and traditional gospel music, applying creative lyric writing from a unique point of view and unclichéd gospel chords that contained his postmodern harmonic tastes. But to me the song, particularly its vocals, didn't develop. It started strong and hit the chorus ("How about love?") great, but then its musical growth became stunted. The building wasn't fully built by the time we got to the end.

Jonathan and I hadn't talked about the show's score since our early conversation about the makeup of the band. The composer has the right to hear his or her music performed exactly as they wrote it, and I figured if Jonathan wanted me to flesh out his work, he would have brought that up, but since he hadn't, there would be no fleshing out just yet. However, I was confident in my vocal arranging and I knew that I would start asking Jonathan if it was okay to try some ideas once we started rehearsal.

I began teaching the song and after we got through the first verse and chorus I had a little sidebar with Jonathan and Michael. I said to Jonathan, "Hey, man, we have twelve singers here. Do you mind if I do a three-part harmony, a contemporary gospel thing in the chorus? I think it may sound fuller and really announce the message of the song." Yes, it was still a delicate conversation to have with a new collaborator, but we didn't have the luxury of a lot of rehearsal time. And I was confident in that what I heard in my head was right for the moment and the song. To my pleasant surprise, Jonathan said, "Sure, let's try it," and when we did, it sounded good.

When we got to the last chorus, I asked Dierdre Boddie-Henderson, our "Seasons of Love" soloist, if she could riff up high, on top of the female group vocals, in a kind of call-and-response to the lyric "remember the love," and do that three times. It was kind of lame, but Jonathan, Michael, and I felt that the song needed a climax, and that's the best I could come up with on short notice. Dierdre sang beautifully, but since Jonathan hadn't written any specific lyrics to end the song, we were left with the call-and-response riffs and a held note at the end, a descant, under which the cast finished out the song. But at least it was in the appropriate place to give the song its climactic ending, hopefully punctuated by applause, so we could proceed cleanly into the next song. That ending, while not completely satisfying, was an important step in the development of "Seasons of Love."

Beyond that and "Seasons of Love B," which was essentially the same vocal arrangement, there wasn't a whole lot of vocal arranging for me to do. Instead my job, first and foremost, was to teach the twelve-member cast Jonathan's unusually long and detailed score. The heavy lift of this task was always present in my mind until I was able to get into a good teaching groove with the cast. During that entire rehearsal and production—a period of a little over a month—Michael and I barely said a dozen words to each other. I think Michael was leaving me alone and trusting me. He knew I had an unusually overwhelming amount of music to teach in a short amount of time, and that I hadn't even gotten to band rehearsals.

Then came week three of our rehearsal period, when I started with the band. We had just one of each instrument in our rhythm section, and just one musician for each. So one guitarist, Dan Carter; one bassist, Chris Berger; and one drummer, Jeff Potter; and me on keyboards. In addition to Jeff's regular drum kit, he also brought in his electronic rig, which produced all the non–drum kit sounds: bongos, congas, electronic bass drums, snares, and tom-toms, a gong, castanets, a vibraslap, cabasa, and concert chimes (think tubular bells). Jeff's programming chops and creativity shone brightly in the song "Light My Candle." I had suggested to Jonathan that the percussion should have a sexier, more rhythmic and urban approach, like Mimi herself, rather than the loop that he and Steve put on his studio demo. Again I stepped out on a limb there with Jonathan, but it didn't seem to bother him. His and Steve's concept wasn't bad—it just didn't have a dramatic point of view. It sounded a little wacky and generic to me. My idea was to have it sound more industrial, reflecting all the twenty-four-seven construction noise in New York City. The drum loop I heard in my head was Prince's "When Doves Cry," with different sounds. Again Jonathan gave the go-ahead. Jeff and I talked about it, and what he brought in was spot-on: a similar rhythm to the Prince tune, with a little agogo bell sprinkled in to give it some Afro-Latin *sabor*, another nod to Mimi. Jeff's execution was way beyond what I had hoped for, and Jonathan liked it.

As far as my own equipment, my keyboard-conductor rig consisted of two keyboards mounted on two parallel tiers and a lot of rack-mounted synthesizers. The rack-mounted pieces could do everything a synthesizer with a keyboard could do, except they didn't come with an actual keyboard. It was just the brains and circuitry of a synthesizer, all neatly fitted into a rectangular box. Since every box had the same width, each of the individual synth "boxes" would be screwed and mounted securely in a protective rack. Hence the term "rack-mounted synths." They could all be connected to each other through a universal connectivity standard known as Musical Instrument Digital Interface, or MIDI. That technology was the basis for all electronic music made after it appeared on the scene. I remember thinking how complicated it seemed when it first showed up in the mid-1980s, but at the end of the day it was just a plug that allowed all my gear to "talk" to each other, making layered sounds that had been impossible to construct in the 1970s. Even with all that technology, the only two of us who could do everything the show demanded were Jeff and Chris. I knew even then that we needed another guitar player and keyboard player, but the Workshop couldn't afford it. We would do as much as we could with what we had.

The music came to us *sort of* orchestrated. Steve had sent his electronically generated files from Jonathan's studio demos to a copyist, who had printed them out and assigned them to each instrument in the manner they deemed most sensible. That plan wasn't ideal because the printouts weren't entirely accurate—there was a fair amount of cutting, pasting, and rewriting that we'd have to do—but the copyist's efforts were helpful and I knew we'd figure it out. My idea was to build each song from the bottom up. Drums and bass, then guitar and keyboards, and everyone in the band would have a creative stake in the outcome. That's what makes a band a band. Through our collective creativity, we would flesh out the songs that needed more creative attention into a musically cohesive whole.

My approach was to start globally, and then as everyone got more familiar with each song I'd make more specific suggestions and everyone would fill out the rest. As we got toward the end of "Christmas Bells," for example, I suggested we approach it like "Bohemian Rhapsody." For "Out Tonight," I thought the best approach was to treat it as a classic seventies rock song. I gave Dan very specific places to play guitar fills in the choruses, as a call-and-response to Mimi's vocals. The drum part all looked the same on paper, so Jeff and I built in more structural elements to his part, loosening up the high hat in the intro, then tightening it up when Mimi started singing the verse. The result was a louder, grungier sound in the intro and a tighter, more classic groove in the verse. To separate the chorus from the verse, I asked Jeff to lean on his ride cymbal. I was giving the band the CliffsNotes version—shorthand ideas that we all knew and understood, which was made easier by Jonathan's taut song structure.

As I saw it there were two questions to consider in the fusion of a rock band and the demands of the theater: how do we play the important things that the cast needed to hear (the piano and guitar for pitch, and the bass and drums for rhythm), and how do we fill out the less fleshed-out music we had received from the copyist? Unlike a traditional Broadway orchestra where the score is read exactly as each note is written, the way a rhythm section works is fundamentally different. There are musical shortcuts and long-held traditions that give the drummer, bassist, and guitarist just enough information for them to understand what to play note-perfect, and where they could stretch out a little. That may mean the player is looking at chords instead of notes or repeat signs instead of longhand notation. In our case, those basic guidelines allowed the band to exert more creative freedom when necessary. In the end it all came down to taste, and I was the final arbiter of that. The one thing that had to be executed exactly as it was given to me was the piano playing, because Jonathan had written it with intention. That meant that the majority of what I would play was what he played on his demos, note for note. The other requirement for the *Rent* band was that the music had to be played the same way every night, so everyone—cast, band, and whoever was calling the show's cues—knew what to expect. This meant we each had to create music that was repeatable for every performance. The variation of a note or a rhythm here or there would be fine, as long as it didn't upset the greater whole.

Remarkably, after a few days we had gotten through the whole score. The show was more than three hours long. That's a heck of a lot of music and was quite an accomplishment for the four of us, given the circumstances. The show was chock full of different musical styles: classic rock, post-punk, power pop, emo, R & B, gospel, and even some jazz. Jonathan knew what he wanted his musical to sound like, and he learned what he *didn't* want his musical to sound like. Eventually he told me, "Those jazzier songs don't fit. They sound great, but that's not the style of the show." He was right. It wasn't difficult to hear, even in rehearsal, that the jazz stuff was like a pair of tan shoes worn with a black tuxedo. A bad match.

We got through rehearsals with the cast, the band, and the cast and band together, as well as tech (short for technical) rehearsals. One day during tech, I walked onto the stage and noticed a stand with a boom and a mic angled at me from the northeast corner of my keyboard rig.

"What's that?" I asked.

Sue White, our production manager, told me, "This is a nonprofit theater. We don't have understudies."

I knew what that meant, even though Sue had said what she said in her succinct, no-nonsense manner. We were doing a musical in a nonprofit theater that had used up its tiny budget, so there were no understudies. She didn't have to say it out loud. I understood her perfectly: be prepared to sing, Tim.

"You're kidding, right?"

"Nope."

To my relief everyone stayed healthy for those two weekends of performances. We did a weekend of shows, had a day off, then worked three more days to rehearse before the following weekend of performances. During that second weekend of shows, I asked my friend Lonny Price, who was a smart and talented director, if he'd come down, look at the show, and tell me what he thought about it. I wasn't sure if I wanted to continue working my ass off for almost no money. My entire salary amounted to barely over a month's rent. Lonny had had a successful acting career (he was in the original cast of Sondheim's infamous musical *Merrily We Roll Along*, as well as the film *Dirty Dancing*, playing the role of Neil Kellerman), and had gone on to become a successful director. He knew theater and its history down to the tiniest detail and could pick apart what made a show good or not. He knew a good song when he heard one, and good dramatic structure when he saw and heard it. Asking for another set of trusted eyes and ears wasn't something I had ever done before, but I had no objectivity with this production and I wasn't smart enough yet to see from the inside if it was good or not. I just knew it was *long*.

I told him, "The show's kind of a mess and it's over three

hours, but I like the composer a lot and he's got a real original voice. He knows Sondheim and pop, which you know is where I live. Would you mind coming down and taking a look at it?"

Lonny and I had done a handful of shows together (including *Sally Marr . . . and Her Escorts*), and I trusted him completely. Since I was seriously considering moving on from the show, I wanted Lon's thoughts about it before I made my decision. Truthfully, I was seriously considering leaving New York. I'd had a pretty good run for the prior fifteen years or so, but what was it adding up to? I didn't know, so I was beginning to look for other career options. Since I wasn't a New Yorker by birth and had no family ties to the area, I was open to anywhere else in the country. I did have a New Yorker's bias about the city and all it offered, especially for artists, but no attachment beyond that. In fact, I had already started looking for teaching jobs around the country through professional artist publications and newsletters.

It turned out that Jonathan was at a similar crossroads. In one of our conversations he shared that if *Rent* didn't go anywhere, he wasn't sure what he was going to do. His day-to-day was waking up, drinking tea, and writing songs—either as stand-alone ones or as part of musical he was working on—then later in the day he would wait tables, most recently at the Moondance Diner. He'd begun to wonder around his thirtieth birthday (he was thirty-four when we started working together) what it was all adding up to. He was broke and most everyone in his close circle of friends was getting married, starting families, and well on their way to having satisfying, successful, money-making careers. We both grew up in the suburbs, so we knew there were alternatives to the lives we were trying to carve out in New York. As a matter of fact, he told me, he had written a one-man show with a few songs reflecting those feelings he was having. "I'd love to hear them sometime," I said.

Lonny did come down to see the show that second week, and

as we had a cigarette during intermission, I asked him what he thought of the first act. He waited a moment, looked me straight in the eye, and said, "Don't you ever quit this show. If you leave it, not only will you be sorry, but I'll never speak to you again."

"What do you mean?" I asked.

"Tim, you're doing *A Chorus Line*," he said, by which he meant that this musical was going to be a once-in-a-generation phenomenon. The fact that he told me this after seeing only the messy, convoluted first act blew my mind.

"Wait until act two," I told him. "It's way clearer. The songs are better and you'll have a more complete idea of it all."

"I don't need to see act two. I've already seen enough to know," he said firmly.

Of course he stayed for the second act, and he remained as sure as he was after the first. He knew the show had, besides its many great songs and the building blocks of a solid structure, that special *something*. He knew it had the magic dust sprinkled on it. Lonny had seen a version of almost every show in the history of musical theater, and he knew intellectually and intuitively what made a show bad, average, good, great, and generation-defining. In the relatively short history of modern musical theater, there were very few shows that could reasonably claim the title of generational. *Company* was one. *A Chorus Line* was another. Was he saying that our three-hour, often messy show would be *that*? Okay, I thought, *I'll see this through for as long as it goes and if it doesn't go anywhere I'll think about my next move, not my next show.* Playing into my need for stability was that, unlike Jonathan, I was married at the time, so I had to think about my wife's needs too. She was having a rough time breaking through as a performer and was open to the idea of living somewhere else, maybe closer to her family in Jackson, Tennessee. But that conversation with Lonny kept me focused on what I was doing in the present, and whatever the next step forward might be with

MAKING RENT
(45)

Rent, I would stay committed to it.

Our brief run finished up the following Sunday. The production was fulfilling in that everyone on the creative team came away with a great feel for what the show looked and sounded like. Although I would have liked to have had another band member or two, the four of us did the job. We made great music together and provided the foundation and support the cast could rely upon. I took mental notes of what I could improve, especially with a few group vocals, and I jotted down some suggestions that I'd make to Jonathan if we ever went forward with another production.

Jonathan was ecstatic. In the short time I had known him, I had never seen him so happy. The show he'd been working on by himself for more than three years finally got up in front of the public. He was thrilled with the audience's response and he seemed satisfied with his own output. After all his painstaking, difficult, and lonely creative work, he had a right to feel as good as he did. He was downright euphoric. Floating on a cloud.

To put as great a finishing touch on this process as one could imagine, we did an all-night marathon recording session of the show at a studio in SoHo. We started around 8:00 p.m. and went straight through until eight the following morning. We did it all, top to bottom, with Steve Skinner producing. There was a lot to do in a relatively short amount of time: no overdubbing, no mixing, just straight to a two-track recorder. There was no time to catch your breath, just the next chord. We ate pizza between tunes. At 9:00 a.m., Dan Carter and I walked out into the daylight and shared a cab to the Upper West Side, where we both lived. I remember squeezing all our gear into a checker cab (spacious, and now sadly obsolete) and heading uptown, tired yet fulfilled, with the cab fare being our only payment for the recording session. In those days, doing an entire demo in a real studio was rare and costly, especially in the early stages of a production, and I was jacked up about the whole experience. Whatever happened or didn't happen to *Rent*, I had a well-produced recording of the entire show on two cassettes.

At the session I'd met a guy who looked around my age and we'd talked for a bit. His name was Kevin McCollum and he was the one financing the session. Little did I know that he had been at the show with his soon-to-be producing partner, Jeffrey Seller. Jeffrey had seen some of Jonathan's previous work before *Rent*, so when he read that Jonathan had a new show at NYTW, he came down. He loved it, and he returned the following night with Kevin accompanying him. By the end of just the first act, Kevin was already crazy about the show. At intermission they found Jonathan and introduced themselves. Kevin literally took out his checkbook right there and said, "How much do you need?" That's how excited a lot of people were about the show. Jonathan's work touched people. His voice as a songwriter was fresh and thrilling. Even though I didn't know Michael that well yet, the originality and creativity of his direction were in sync with Jonathan's vision. Add to that the energy pouring off the stage from the cast and band, and it all added up to a very soulful and satisfying night at the theater. Kevin and Jeffrey saw the show multiple times and brought others downtown throughout our short run.

Later I would find out that after Kevin and Jeffrey met Jonathan, they introduced him to the well-known entertainment lawyer and Broadway producer Jay Harris, who agreed to provide Jonathan with legal representation. Kevin and Jeffrey would come aboard as commercial producers, along with NYTW, and Kevin would finance the recording session. Once Jonathan told me about what was going on, I was so happy for him. His dreams were starting to come to life, and I was grateful to be a part of it. For me the best news came with the announcement that there would be a full production of *Rent* the following year at NYTW, and Jonathan and Michael want-

MAKING RENT

ed me to stay on as musical director. While it would only be a six-week run, pretty much the average for a theater producing a full season of shows, it felt momentous, and I thought maybe there would be an extension if tickets sold well. Either way, the news meant I had work scheduled a year ahead of time, a first for me. In my mind, due mostly to Lonny's strong persuasion, I was already committed to this project, no matter the outcome. I didn't have any delusions though. There was still a long road ahead and the history of musical theater told us that the odds of a show having any kind of commercial success weren't favorable. And in the meantime I still had to make a living, so while I waited to return to *Rent*, I went back to subbing shows, dry-cleaning the tuxedo, and playing club dates from Poughkeepsie to Bangor. The show had been a great experience, and though there was more on the horizon, for now it stopped as abruptly as it had begun.

Richard Rodgers was one of the most influential composers the musical theater world has ever known. For six decades in the twentieth century his compositions were an essential part of American musical theater. His work was the beating heart of the Great American Songbook from the 1920s to the 1970s. The prestigious Richard Rodgers Awards for Musical Theater, which was developed in 1978, gives grants to musical theater writers annually. The artist receives a sum of money, one-third of which goes to them and two-thirds of which goes to a nonprofit theater, where the work had to be produced during that theater's following season.

In early 1994 Jonathan Larson was one of the recipients of the award for his submission of *Rent*. His prize was $45,000. Since Jonathan had done his 1993 reading of *Rent* at NYTW, it was a natural fit (and a condition of the grant) that the 1994 production would happen there as well. Without that money, the New York Theater Workshop would never have been able to finance our 1994 production. If that production hadn't happened, it's anyone's guess as to the future and fate of *Rent*.

Michael, Jonathan, and Marlies in rehearsal at the New York Theatre Workshop, 1995.

NEXT STEPS
1995

THE REST OF NOVEMBER AND DECEMBER came and went. Fortunately, from the beginning of December through New Year's Eve, the gigs were plentiful if one was doing club dates and subbing, like I was. There were lots of holiday parties, and Broadway musicians were taking more time off to be with their families. Even though I knew there would be a production of *Rent* later the next year, there was still a long way to go before then and *my* rent wasn't waiting. I had been in New York for a good twelve years by then, so I had been woven more into the fabric of the music and theater scene, met more people who hired me, and worked enough to get by. I came off my *Rent* experience feeling more confident, and I felt that translated into my doing higher-quality work. My private coaching business started to improve as mysteriously as it had vaporized, and some gigs other than club dates materialized: rock and blues gigs, arranging opportunities, a recording session every so often, and even some backup jingle singing. I could sing well enough, but the real key was that I could sight-read. Gratefully, I was hired by a couple of friendly jingle producers who knew I was struggling financially. Into my theater life came another reading here, another workshop there, all with the hope that something would break through, as was my hope for *Rent*. Really, I cobbled together a living best as I could, like always. Through a good friend, I even started writing songs and singing for a few cartoon shows.

In January 1995, NYTW came back into full production mode for its upcoming season. Jim's work as artistic director was to get everything organized from the top down. He had to delegate and secure the production staff, crew, and casting directors for the season. A couple of their plays kept their casts intact from previous readings, which was common. But they did have a new play, and now a musical to cast. The play was Doug Wright's *Quills*, which was transferring from the Woolly Mammoth Theatre Company in Washington, DC, to the Workshop. The musical, of course, was *Rent*. As demanding a task as it was to put *Rent* on the stage in 1994, this upcoming production would require a more fully realized version of itself. Jonathan and Michael had always envisioned a larger cast, so they landed on fifteen actors. Michael knew what was required to meet the needs of Jonathan's show, and Jim knew how many actors the theater's space could accommodate offstage, so that number was the compromise Michael, Jonathan, and Jim agreed upon. Jonathan would have preferred a large opera company, rock band, and full orchestra, but that wasn't happening. Instead, I would be able to hire a fifth musician.

Jonathan, understandably, was feeling pretty good about the piece (and himself) after the success of 1994, but Jim and Michael weren't quite as satisfied. What I didn't fully understand at the time was that Jim and Michael's knowledge of storytelling, plot, and structure (not to mention their great taste and aesthetics) was, like my friend Lonny's, high-end. So when Jonathan came into Jim's office and announced he felt his work was complete and he felt great about the show, Jim's response was "No, it's not done, and here are the reasons why."

That was a tense time for the collaboration between Jonathan and the Workshop. Jim told Jonathan that his work was still too general. It wasn't character or plot-driven enough, and his storytelling was still at times vague and needed to be much clearer. The multiple stories of the many people's lives he was telling needed to be more focused on their journeys individually, as couples, as part of larger friend groups, and so on. Jim suggested that Jonathan would benefit greatly if he worked with a dramaturge to help him further flesh out his characters and their stories. A dramaturge (from the Greek word *dramatourgos*, which roughly means "drama work") helps clarify the drama in a theatrical work. Jim and Michael wanted someone to help Jonathan refine his storytelling for this new, fifteen-character version of *Rent*. After a lot of back-and-forth, Lynn Thompson was brought on board. Jim thought she and Jonathan would be a great fit. Lynn was a well-established dramaturge, director, and professor who had worked up and down the East Coast for many years and had been a vital part of NYC's downtown theater scene for a long time. She was someone who Jim trusted would be of important service to Jonathan and his work. Bringing in Lynn was also kind of an ultimatum from the Workshop—either Jonathan agreed to this, or they would reconsider producing his show altogether. That development certainly punctured his tires, but to his credit, he agreed. In addition to having creative instincts, Jonathan also possessed the practical instinct of wanting to get his show up, however that had to happen.

Bernie Telsey had owned and run a small casting office in New York since 1988. He and his partners, Will Cantler and David Vaccari, were a three-person operation, and they were a ferocious team. Bernie had previously paid his dues as a casting director for seven years, mostly while working under the well-known and beloved casting agent Meg Simon. In Bernie's partnership with Will and David, each brought their own specialties: David was a great casting director for commercials, like Bernie, while Bernie and Will had expertise in the theater. Will was an accomplished director in his own right, and he and Bernie had cast many shows for the prestigious Goodman Theatre in Chicago, as well as Hartford Stage in Connecticut. Will was also one of the resident directors at a noted off-Broadway theater, the Manhattan Class Company (MCC), so Bernie suggested he should direct the commercials they were casting. A very nice parlay for their small company. Soon they were doing lots of commercials, and they would cast them from the huge pool of actors from MCC, with Will directing. The three men had an industrious, unrelenting work ethic, and as a result they were starting to become very successful for such a small operation (they should've called themselves MCC, the Maniacal Casting Company). Sharing their love for the theater, Bernie, Will, and Robert LuPone (the late brother of Patti LuPone and a great actor who later played Tony Soprano's neighbor, Bruce Cusamano, on *The Sopranos*) eventually took over as the artistic directors of MCC, which grew to new heights, in a similar vein to what Jim Nicola was doing down at NYTW.

One day Bernie got a call from the famous avant-garde theater director Peter Sellars (not to be confused with the actor Peter Sellers). Bernie knew Peter from his many years with Meg Simon, who had moved into television casting. Peter asked Bernie if he would cast a production of Shakespeare's *The Merchant of Venice* at the Goodman Theatre, as well as a new rock opera he was directing after that. The latter would have to be cast with rock and R & B singer-actors. It was written by John Adams (the famous composer, not the president). Adams had written the contemporary opera *Nixon in China*, which, even before its debut in 1987, was highly visible in the arts world. It was, unlike most operas, topical and American, so the interest and scrutiny of the piece were intense. It opened at the Houston Grand Opera to mixed reviews and ultimately didn't live up to the hype. The things that were groundbreaking about the opera were the things that kept the opera critics at bay. There were so many musical influences in its score, way beyond the traditional boundaries of opera: jazz, swing-era big band music, percussion, and other music way outside the classical tradition, like pop, R & B, and Latin—with synthesizers no less. Electronic music in the opera? While unapologetically avant-garde and groundbreaking for its time, *Nixon in China* was like a bad kid doing doughnuts on his bike through the manicured shrubs and gardens of the opera neighborhood.

Adams's new rock opera was titled *I Was Looking at the Ceiling and Then I Saw the Sky,* and Sellars told Bernie that it was going to change the world. Since the two of them were friends and professional peers, Bernie decided that he would take on the project. It was, at that time, an uncommon casting responsibility. Bernie couldn't simply call on his theater people who could sing pop—Sellars and Adams wanted authentic rock and rollers and R & B singers plucked from the theater's underbelly: the clubs, community centers, and off-the-grid places where so many great singers (and hopefully actors) were plying their trade. Since it was going to be a European, nonunion tour, the idea of *I Was Looking at the Ceiling* coming to New York was not on the table and therefore a huge disincentive for an actor who might otherwise take the gig. The project was an uphill climb for Bernie and he hated every minute of it. Yet, being the casting lunatic that he was, he took on the task, which beat him to a pulp.

In late 1994 the opera did end up coming to New York City for two tired weeks at a little-known theater on the Upper West Side. Downtown, Jim Nicola knew that the upcoming 1995–96 production of *Rent* would need a heavy dose of contemporary singers. So when he heard about *I Was Looking at the Ceiling* he went to check it out. Wendy Ettinger, our casting director in 1994, had left the business to raise a family, and Bernie's experience with the Adams production would be invaluable in casting *Rent*.

NYTW had gained a lot of stature in the downtown theater scene, which was in Bernie's comfort zone. Before *Rent* in that upcoming season was *Quills*. Bernie had read and loved the play but had absolutely no idea what *Rent* was. He listened ambivalently to a couple of the demo songs we had recorded. He knew that Michael had directed a play at MCC but knew nothing else about him, and he didn't know *Rent* or Jonathan. This wasn't a surprise, as we were still a micro-dot on the NYC theater scene, and that's a generous description.

When Jim called Bernie and made his offer, Bernie responded by asking, "Is there any way I could just do *Quills*?"

"I want you to cast *Quills* and *Rent*," Jim responded. "It's either both of them or neither of them." There was Jim in his role as artistic director, putting his marker down, dropping the hammer on Bernie, offering a take-it-or-leave-it deal, a risk he was willing to take. Bernie, still suffering from the scars of the John Adams musical, accepted the entire package, despite his misgivings. *Another rock opera that would change the world*, he thought sarcastically, but he said to himself, *You just don't fucking say no*. That was his approach. A real dog.

As the calendar turned to 1995, Michael was beginning his job as the new artistic director of the La Jolla Playhouse, located just north of downtown San Diego. The theater, because of its rich history and proximity to Los Angeles, had become one of the most popular regional theaters in the country. Due to its esteemed leadership and the frequency of high-quality artistic directors working there, as well as its facilities and beautiful location on the campus of the University of California San Diego, La Jolla was then, and remains today, one of the go-to theaters for plays and musicals that had their sights set on commercial success. Almost three dozen of its plays and musicals had successfully transferred to Broadway since the 1980s, and the theater itself won a Tony Award as one of the country's most outstanding regional theaters. Needless to say, Michael couldn't have passed up that gig. While he was beginning his tenure there, the casting wheels were starting to turn back in New York. Beginning in March of 1995, Bernie brought Jonathan and me in for vocal auditions, with Michael flying in once a month for the callbacks of the singers we had approved.

The first appointment on the first day Jonathan and I came in was with a young man named Taye Diggs. He had recently finished the musical *Carousel*, which had a successful run at Lincoln Center and starred another promising newcomer, Audra McDonald. Taye was a dancer who sang well, and he was good-looking, charming, and soulful. Jonathan and I liked him immediately. Jonathan didn't have the "That's Mark!" type of reaction he'd had in the 1994 audition of Anthony, but we both had a very good gut feeling. Ultimately Michael would have to sign off on Taye as well, but it was an encouraging start.

Then the process got harder, and harder. We went through a long series of auditions where we didn't like many, or any, of the singers who came in. They didn't have a good sense of rock or R & B rhythm, attitude, or feel. A lot of the auditioners didn't listen to, or had never studied, popular music. Instead they had absorbed and studied traditional theater music, which was the music of their chosen profession. It wasn't their fault that they couldn't fit into our sound and approach, but we knew that singers who understood, felt, and could sing music in the way Jonathan and I heard it were out there somewhere. I was still doing gigs in the city's clubs, so I heard a lot of them and even asked a few if they'd like to audition. None were interested in doing a musical.

That routine plodded on through the early spring months, with Michael flying in every four to six weeks, whenever he could get away. Bernie was frustrated with the lack of success, but he put his frustration to good use. Typically, casting directors sent breakdowns of the characters to agents and managers, providing genders, vocal requirements, and, in the case of *Rent*, the emphasis on multiethnicity. A good number of agents submitted their clients and when they did it was hit-or-miss whether the client would even show up for their audition. A rock opera at an unknown nonprofit theater in the East Village? Low pay? Long hours? No thank you, they seemed to say collectively. Realizing that traditional casting was a failed mission, Bernie, Will, and David had to think of other methods to find the nontraditional performers they knew were out there. Somewhere.

Besides running audition notices in the well-established theatrical trade magazines *Backstage* and *Show Business*, they put up signs at YMCAs, community centers, community swimming pools, and smaller, lesser-known theaters way, *way* off Broadway. Since we needed Latin men and women, they went into the Latin communities, particularly the Washington Heights neighborhood of Upper Manhattan, and at Intar, a Midtown Manhattan theater dedicated to Latin productions (think NYTW, only the fully Latin version). They put up flyers at all the city colleges in Brooklyn, Queens, and Staten Island, and even at the Boston Conservatory and Carnegie Mellon in Pittsburgh. The net was cast far and wide, and since they had little to no money for their casting budget, their process was old-school: take the subway, put up a sign or three, then get back on the subway. Rinse and repeat, all day every day. I called Bernie the "king of creativity," but he called himself the "king of desperation." Man, those guys were *game* to take on the challenge and embraced it with unflagging thought, vigor, and enthusiasm, trying every method under the sun despite having limited funds. They did have lots of quarters for the pay phones though, an integral part of their guerilla casting process.

We already had Anthony, Gilles, and Daphne, despite Jonathan's insistence that Bernie continue to audition her. Poor Daphne. But she kept returning and didn't show any resentment or attitude about being called back in, a real sign of her inner strength and thick skin. Whenever she had to, she came in and did her thing—beautifully. Again and again. I had given up even talking to Jonathan about her. He knew how I felt. She had already proven herself in the 1994 production, so case closed as far as I was concerned.

It was during those months in 1995 that Jonathan and I hung out a little more, just having a beer or glass of wine, talking about work, about art in general and theater in particular. They weren't like the conversations we'd had in college, not least because for both of us that was almost a half lifetime ago. In college my roommate and I would meet up at the end of each day, get stoned, listen to music, light cockroaches on fire, and consume cinnamon toast by the loaf. The conversations would always skew toward art and the world, and all our developing opinions on it, however naive or immature. We had endless heart-to-hearts about being an artist, the incalculable value of music to society, and the merits of learning to improvise (me) versus the merits of learning trombone orchestral excerpts that were a necessary part of becoming a serious classical musician (him). And sure enough, Jonathan had had his version of those conversations with his roommate and good friend Todd Robinson, with whom he'd spent three years at Adelphi University and was still close. Their conversations, he told me, were more theater-centric, but they too devoured music in large gulps and talked about the conditions surrounding their artistry and the world at large.

My conversations with Jonathan, just over fifteen years removed from college, had a different tenor to them. We were both youngish professionals in New York's performing arts scene in some way or another, but we were in different places, sort of. Despite the recurring ups and downs I was going through financially, I was having more professional (paid) success as a musician. Unlike Jonathan, I didn't have to hold on to a "regular" job, except for a handful of months right after I arrived in 1982. I made enough to get by most of the time. Jonathan had been working at the diner five or six shifts a week for the previous ten years. Despite his relative financial success as an up-and-coming young writer in the theater, winning small grants and earning some commissions for his work, the art form that he was mastering was songwriting, which was difficult enough in and of itself, and on top of that he was trying to be a songwriter in the musical theater. "If this was easy, more people would be doing it," he said to me. This was even harder when coupled with the fact that he was trying to write *pop-rock* music for the theater, where historically music had rarely come with a solid backbeat, so he was trying, on multiple levels and for many years, to crack multiple codes.

As up and down and as hopeful or melancholy as he'd been about his chosen life's work, I could see he was resolute about his professional goals, most importantly bringing the younger generation into the theater that he loved. His occasional depression was far outweighed by his willfulness, his frustration offset by his ferocity. I came to understand and respect what he was doing, and even though neither of us knew what the future held for *Rent*, the fact that he was making progress on it at all strengthened his resolve. I thought he was more passionate about his work than I was about mine. I thought he was more unwavering and undaunted about what he wanted to achieve than I was. What I took away from all those conversations were two main truths. One: in the musical theater, players play and writers write. And two: while anyone can learn to play an instrument, songwriting is *hard*. In fact, it's heroic, and it was the efforts by songwriters in music and the musical theater, like Jonathan, that gave folks like me a place to go, a place to work. My respect for him and his work had grown exponentially from the first time we had met eight or nine months prior. He was also charming, funny, and smart—whip-smart. Even though I was working with and for him, I genuinely liked the guy. In my music and theater career thus far, that had rarely been the case. And beyond being one likable human being, he was one serious artist.

While the casting process continued, we all started discussing more specifically who these characters were. Did Mimi and Angel have to be Latin? Yes. Did Roger have to be white? With all due respect to Lenny Kravitz, probably yes. Did Collins have to be white, like Pat Briggs from the 1994 production? Not necessarily. What did we want the homeless community to look like? We wanted it to look like the East Village. White, Black, Latin, Asian, older, younger, bigger, smaller—no limits or requirements. Since the homeless population was made up of such a cross section of humanity, Michael, Jonathan, and Jim especially wanted to make sure that the characters weren't caricatures. Who were these people? Some may have chosen that life clearly and rationally, maybe others were mentally ill, and some were just plain broke (something not uncommon in New York). What they shared was dignity, and they deserved respect. In the auditions Michael was looking for actors who brought a kind of wisdom, an understanding of the wider world they were living in, a society much broader and more diverse than the sometimes narrow world felt by a performer. How would they bring that awareness to the audition experience? Michael and Bernie were especially good at sensing if someone had this quality. Jonathan and I were more concerned about getting the right singers, and I was focused on making sure we were getting an appropriate balance of voices: baritones, tenors, altos, and sopranos. We needed enough of each to cover the musical terrain of the show.

We eventually started seeing the right talent over those next few months, but until we were all in the audition room together, nothing could be set in stone. It wouldn't be until September that we'd begin to nail down our cast. If we cast someone in the early spring, it would be a crapshoot. They could easily get a better offer over the next six months, they'd take it, and who could blame them? Then for Bernie it would be back to the pay phones. I thought if all we got from those auditions was Taye, that would be fine. Bernie, Will, and David would keep doing their thing and it would bear fruit in the early autumn.

Part of what was most interesting to me about the auditions where Michael was present was watching his process. The actors would come in and do the performative part of their audition, introducing themselves and what they were about to sing—standard stuff. Maybe there would be a little small talk and then they would sing their audition material. Michael would give them a note or two and if they showed they understood the note and made an adjustment the second time around, he would continue to engage them with a little conversation, not necessarily about the show or show business, or maybe a little joke. From my limited experience, every director had their own way of finding out what they liked. Whatever their own personal checklist was, they mined it during the auditions and callbacks. I still didn't know Michael very well at the time, but I learned that he had a deep understanding of human behavior and group dynamics. I was finding out his likes and dislikes, his red flags, and his personal tastes. He wanted to be sure the actors, like the creative team, were reliable partners. I learned a lot from watching and participating in auditions with Michael.

My own vocal requirements for those who came in weren't just about their pitch. I needed to assess how their voices would hold up three hours each night, eight times a week. If I had concerns, not unlike Michael, I would give them vocal adjustments or exercises and see how well they responded to my vocal notes. The thing I knew was they had to have a technique that, over time, would prove dependable. I wasn't a professional voice teacher in any respect, but I knew my stuff. The suggestions I gave were more practical than anything, so they were easy enough to digest. I emphasized the value of consonants, which would take the stress off their vocal cords and focus their energy on the clarity of Jonathan's lyrics. However, the thing that mattered to me most, that others in my position paid less attention to, was their sense of time. Did they have good rhythm, feel, and groove? Did they rush, even slightly, when they were singing louder, or drag when they were singing softer? Could they hold a steady tempo without an accompaniment? If someone had bad time they weren't getting past me. I didn't care if they sounded like Pavarotti. No time, no hire.

Maybe because the stakes weren't so high for an unknown musical at a little-known theater the actors seemed less nervous, or maybe they were an unusual bunch who were comfortable in their own skin. I liked them all, even though we wouldn't call most of them back. Many of them were smart, funny, open, and decent. Michael habitually searched for the uniqueness in everyone we saw. As a group I knew we were different from every creative team I had previously been a part of. We were a patient bunch, all of us behind the table. Part of that was out of necessity, but as a unit, with Michael setting the overall tone, our kindness never wavered. Bernie, Will, and David's commitment to their nontraditional casting process carried each day we were together, and what became clear was that we were firmly on our way to hiring a talented and multiethnic, multiracial community of performers.

Once the first batch of auditions ended in the late spring of 1995, the safe haven of theater gave way to the full-time reality that the life I had built was full-time crumbling. My marriage had been on the rocks for some time, but my wife and I had been ignoring the issues. And mostly we ignored them by drinking. My drink of choice was a shot of Kentucky bourbon dropped into a glass of English stout. Partnered with my drinking was a lifelong, off-and-on—more on than off—smoking habit. Still, even with those indulgences, most mornings I'd go for a six-mile run around Central Park, and whatever gig was coming, I showed up and did it. Being uber-responsible professionally and taking a daily run was a direct response to the chaos of my world. My career was on life support, my marriage was barely twitching, and my bad habits were my closest allies. I was just trying to counterbalance it all with something.

When my wife and I finally acknowledged the irreparable state of our marriage, we had to make a plan. I helped her move into an apartment she found and even cosigned her first lease. That was the caretaker in me, always present and accountable. Vouching for her wasn't difficult because we didn't hate each other—we just knew the marriage was over. She was ten years my junior, and the difficulties due to our age gap weren't sustainable. I was grateful it only took us six years to figure that out.

As a result of our breakup, I had to move too, but first I had to put my belongings (including my piano) into storage and find a place to live until I could scrape up enough money for a studio apartment. Soon enough, I rented a small bedroom and bathroom in an apartment on West End Avenue that was owned by the well-known Irish actor Malachy McCourt. (If the last name sounds familiar, it's because his brother, Frank McCourt, wrote the novel *Angela's Ashes*.) It met all my requirements: I could afford the room and it was available.

Running on financial fumes, and with the occasional help of my brother Matt, whose belief in me never wavered, I spent late spring into summer taking hours-long walks around Manhattan, top to bottom, east to west, just as I had when I'd arrived fourteen years earlier. I marveled at how quickly, efficiently, and nonchalantly New York City flipped my life upside down, primarily due to the uncaring financial pressure it put on its inhabitants. The harsh realization that my artistic life wasn't going in anything that resembled a straight line kept gnawing at me. I'd never been

MAKING RENT

without my own home or apartment, which on some level could be applauded, but the unpredictability that now ruled my world was unsettling. Maybe the reason I'd gotten a twenty-year-old college senior pregnant and kept my promise to marry her, despite a miscarriage, was that I wanted a version of the stability that I had grown up with to counteract a life that I knew was unstable by its nature. The joke that your wedding day is such a special occasion that you only do it twice was probably written for artists.

Since I couldn't afford to drink, my thinking became less cluttered and I realized that maybe I was in the midst of a life reset and that my possessions and gigs weren't helping me do that. Spending a few months not thinking about money and gigs (easy to do, since I had neither) turned out to have its own value. I started imagining positive outcomes rather than wallowing in a professional stress that skewed negative, a common bad habit in my profession. The reset was real emotional progress for me and I could feel it, but after two months at Mr. McCourt's apartment, he gave me thirty days to pack up and leave. It must not have sat well that I came and went all hours of the day and night, not in a drunk and scumbaggy way but apparently not without being a disruption to Mr. McCourt and his wife.

Before I had to leave, I was offered a gig in Italy with a USO Broadway-style concert that would perform for US Marines (and their families) stationed around the Italian coast. The gig was unsalaried, and the pay was only to cover my travel, hotel, and a small per diem. I took it primarily because I had nowhere to live, it would kill a month or so, and I could go somewhere I had never been. Thankfully I didn't have to bring my own equipment, so I packed light and off I went.

Ten of us—five singers and five musicians, a couple of whom brought partners or spouses—were on that brief summer tour. Following a series of concerts at the numerous Marine bases that dotted much of the Italian coastline, we were transported from shore to sea via military rafts (gear and all) for our arrival aboard the aircraft carrier USS *George Washington*. Our first performance was planned for that night aboard the ship as it moved farther out into the Adriatic Sea. However, the carrier got orders to prepare a bombing mission aimed at the Bosnian coast, as part of the war that tore Yugoslavia apart in the early nineties. So, instead, we did our show at 7:00 the next morning, and by 10:00 a.m. we had all been slingshotted off the aircraft carrier, like I'd seen on TV news broadcasts so many times. A little Broadway entertainment before a geopolitically significant bombing mission? What, and give up show business? I met some great performers and musicians on that gig, it was good to get out of town, and in addition to touring the Italian coast, I got to experience a bit of an adventure on the back end.

When I got back to New York, the most immediate needs were still waiting: money and a place to crash. Luckily, Lonny said I could stay on his couch for as long as I needed. A godsend. I hooked up my landline and answering machine in his closet, and task one was complete. Lonny's couch was the third of my four residences since the beginning of my life with *Rent*, just over a year-and-a-half before. More and more, especially during the previous months, I came to realize what *Rent* was becoming for me, other than the life-imitating-art part. It was becoming familial. I had gotten closer to Jonathan, Jim, and Bernie, and Michael and we were becoming a nice professional fit, despite the infrequency of his trips back east. Even the folks at the Workshop, upon finding out about my separation, started to ask if they could fix me up. I was a real catch, I told them. Broke *and* homeless. Residence number four would come soonish, thankfully.

Sustained enough by playing club dates and subbing, I started to get back on my feet once again. And in the meantime, the Workshop had scheduled a sing-through of *Rent*, so that everyone could hear the work that Jonathan had written since the end of 1994 with input from Lynn, Michael, and Jim. It wasn't a paying gig, of course, but it was a welcome reminder of what was to come. I felt a familiar warmth and anticipation as I took the subway ride downtown from the Upper West Side. The 1, 2, or 3 train to Forty-Second Street, the transfer through the beginnings of a cleaner and newer Times Square station to the R or N train, down to East Eighth Street and Broadway. I loved getting off at Eighth Street. I had spent so much time down there, whether it was going to record stores, doing gigs, or eating the best Indian food in New York, particularly at the famed restaurants Milon and Panna II. My arrival at NYTW felt like a reunion, where my friends and collaborators from the previous incarnation had gathered.

We all assembled in the rehearsal room and Jonathan put a new song in front of me, titled "Tango: Maureen." It was a good song, and although it was in its early stages, like Jonathan's other work, it was well on its way to being great. He also brought in a new song for Joanne, titled "We're Okay," as well as a duet for Maureen and Joanne called "Love of My Life," which was supposed to be funny, playful, and silly. I didn't think it came off as such, but I could have been wrong. Near the end of the show, Jonathan had made cuts and revisions to "Finale A" and "Finale B." Those were the new songs that I remember from that night, but "Tango: Maureen" was a real sign of what was to come. Between Michael, Lynn, and Jim's suggestions, Jonathan needed to get away from focusing on Mark and Maureen's relationship history and home in on Joanne and Maureen's relationship in the present, getting across that it was serious and meaningful. Funny, yes, but not at all frivolous.

The sing-through went fine. The reaction from those in attendance—Jim, Martha, the rest of the staff at NYTW, Michael, Bernie, Kevin, and Jeffrey—was a little bit of everything. They were all encouraged by the new songs Jonathan had written, yet a little discouraged that the overall work still didn't have enough clarity and focus on the characters or their stories. Jonathan was writing about a lot of individuals, groups of friends, and converging events simultaneously. His musical was a serious undertaking. There were multiple characters and plots and, as I saw it, he just wasn't quite done with it yet. I'd only done a handful of new musicals by that time, but I knew that writers not only had to know the characters they were writing for but also the actual *people* they were writing for. Their voices, rhythms, and manners. I thought Jonathan still had the 1994 cast in his imagination. Clearly good news that came that day was that Michael was returning from La Jolla to New York in September and we would finally cast the 1995–96 production. The natural ratcheting up of pressure of an oncoming production schedule, with some real money on the line, breathed a new sense of urgency into the process. Good urgency.

Before the September auditions began, I had to get a new band in order. Chris Berger, the bass player, had no interest in continuing with the show. Jeff Potter, our drummer, was interested in moving forward with it, which I was happy to hear, and I tasked him with finding a bass player he wanted to play with, who he felt would be a good fit for the show. Then came the hard part. I had been friends with Dan Carter, the guitarist, for about ten years. We had done a lot of gigs and a couple of shows together (I met Dan on *Oh! Calcutta!*). I knew he could play all the different styles in the show, which is why I'd tapped him in 1994. But the truth was, I had more reasons to let him go than to keep him. Despite our personal history, he wasn't the best player for the job. Now that I had a more complete sense of what I wanted the band to sound like, Dan's style, his musical identity, wasn't in that sonic pocket. And while my other reason may seem petty, it was part of my decision-making. Dan was a big dude, and the space he had to live in onstage was tight. His setup included two guitars hung closely next to him, a complete pedalboard at his feet, and his music stand and light. Altogether it made for a tight squeeze, and during the 1994 performances I heard a lot of nonmusical noise as Dan tried to negotiate his environment. It was a big distraction, and I couldn't take that chance again. That was the first time I had to make a decision like that, firing an old friend, but in the end it came down to what was in the show's best interest. It was the embodiment of the axiom "It's not called show *friend*; it's called show *business*."

I called Dan to tell him. He understood, if a bit ruefully. Since he was born and raised in the city, he knew the drill. Before we hung up, though I felt a little awkward, I asked him if he knew anyone who could play keyboards and guitar. In fact, he did. A good friend of his, Dan Weiss, whom I knew from the club date circuit, was available. He said he'd call Dan, tell him about the gig, and give him my number if he was interested. I appreciated that, especially since I'd just fired him in the same conversation. Real generosity from a true friend.

Dan Carter called Dan Weiss, then Dan Weiss called me, and we talked about music in general and what he was working on. I barely knew him. We had played one club date together, where he played bass. My first thought was, *Man, this guy is talented. He plays keyboards, guitar, and bass?* He told me that the club date scene had worn him down to a nub, causing emotional damage, and so he'd decided to hang it up for a while, taking a job at Tekserve, one of the top computer repair shops in New York at the time. I really admired that. Only a self-examined person would experience a problem and do something about it in such a drastic but necessary way. I started talking to him about the theater in general, then got down to the *Rent* situation, where we were in the process, and explained that it would be a five-piece rhythm section. A real band. A scene where we'd all have ownership in the musical outcome of the show. The director and composer—

lyricist took the music and the musicians in the band seriously. And anyway it wasn't a long commitment, so he wouldn't be signing his life away. He said he'd do it. I think part of the appeal for him was that the show sounded exactly like the opposite of his club date life and the disregard for musicians that went with it.

Now I had to find a guitarist. I knew quite a few, but I hit it off best with Kenny Brescia. Kenny was a friendly, smart Jersey guy and a fantastic all-around musician. We had done a handful of corporate gigs together with the Rhythm Dogs and he and I were both subbing at *Tommy*, so I was intimately familiar with his playing. Many of New York's great guitar players subbed on that show and when I was subbing I could hear them blasting through my headphones. Kenny sounded fantastic. I wanted to offer him the gig, but just to be thorough, I needed to have a conversation about all of it in person, to discuss the project, the theater, and the low pay. Kenny's theater experience was limited to *Tommy*, so laying out the whole *Rent* scene would help him better understand the context of my offer.

Coincidentally, he was playing a gig with an Irish singer-songwriter we both knew, so one night in early October I went down to an Irish rock club in the East Village, called Sin-é, to hear them. On a break we stepped outside and I told him what I needed to tell him, then added, "I think you'd be good at this theater th ing." We talked a bit more and then I blurted out, "I think you should do it." I couldn't believe those words came out of my mouth. I wasn't an "I think you should . . ." kind of guy, especially professionally. I was more in the category of "Would you be interested . . . ?" But in that moment, I gave him my opinion straight up. He said yes, and the band was set. I hadn't met the bass player yet, but I trusted Jeff's judgment and taste, so I had no concerns. The biggest concern to all of us was the low pay. But as I had said to Dan, if we could just hang with it for a few months, what could possibly go wrong? I used to joke with the band, "Stick with me, and you'll make in the low-three figures."

Since I was unable to cover all the keyboard parts in the 1994 version and we would now have an additional player, I asked Steve Skinner to separate out all the MIDI files in such a way that the copyists could make two keyboard books. It didn't have to be perfect, I told him. We'd fix it up once we got into band rehearsal. There was plenty of time for that. Our pressing need that fall was a final cast. We still had important slots to fill: Benny, Maureen, Joanne, Collins, Angel, and Roger. And we had to make a decision on Mimi.

I'm happy to say that we did officially cast Daphne as Mimi eventually. She had proven herself over and over, and the truth was that out of the six of us (Bernie, Jim, Martha, Michael, Jonathan, and me), the only one who still might have had a doubt was Jonathan. He finally said yes. Nothing dramatic happened for him to get there. There were no arguments, no ultimatums. I believe that the huge reservoir of trust we'd built up over our past year together and Daphne's undeniable success in the 1994 version all contributed to his agreeing to cast her.

A couple of weeks after Labor Day 1995, we got down to the business of finding those last actors and calling back some of the folks we had seen earlier in the year. We had all liked Taye Diggs back in March and, thankfully, he was available, so he was cast as Benny. His portrayal of Benny at his callback was cool and smooth, savvy and tactical. Also, he was a skilled dancer and our choreographer, Marlies Yearby, who joined us for this final round of auditions, would be able to feature him in the dance-heavy song "Contact," when he wasn't playing Benny. All I cared about was that he could sing and had a voice that could blend easily into an ensemble.

The next order of business was to flesh out who would be playing the members of the homeless community, the support group, and all the other unnamed roles. Bernie, David, and Will delivered, just like I'd thought they would. They were on a serious casting heater. Fantastic actor-singers came in, seemingly one after another, and destroyed. Kristen Lee Kelly was first: an amazing singer with a healthy belt and lovely soprano who carried herself like a real rocker, an appealing blend of qualities for me. Truth was, she was a badass. She and Michael had a little repartee going, and Kristen held her own, funny and sharp. She had the attitude of *This is who I am—any questions?* Next was a young man named Rodney Hicks. I mean, *young*. He was twenty-one at the time, but he looked sixteen. He sang well enough, but since Marlies needed dancers, she asked if he could do anything fun, at which point Rodney did a full standing backflip, landing back on his feet. Good enough for Marlies, and for us.

Another dancer came in, Aiko Nakasone, who had come off a nice run of work: the national tour of *The Who's Tommy* and the out-of-town tryout in La Jolla of the revival of *How to Succeed in Business Without Really Trying*, starring Matthew Broderick, and its subsequent move to Broadway. Michael had seen her in the La Jolla production and he assured Marlies that Aiko could be the foundational presence in her choreography. Since Aiko had just come from Broadway, she was probably making more money on unemployment than she would at the Workshop, but lucky for us she chose the Workshop. For her audition she sang Heart's "Straight On," but she didn't sing it like those Wilson sisters from back in the day; instead, she sang warmly and had solid pitch and time. She was a pro, quietly self-assured. Then Byron Utley, who presented a little older than the rest of the folks we had seen, came in. He looked great, sang great, and seemed completely secure with himself in a very mature way, which is why I thought he was older. It didn't matter. Now that we were viewing the character of Collins as a Black man, Byron would make a great understudy. I thought his sound lent itself well to the male "Seasons of Love" soloist, and I had a plan for a trio in the "I'll Cover

You" reprise that he would fit into nicely. He had a wide vocal range—three-plus octaves, from a true baritone to a second tenor. We were filling slots with talented and interesting people, which was a relief to all of us, but there was still more to do.

We had to find a Maureen, who wasn't yet fully formed as a character, but for whom Michael knew he wanted someone with some smarts, warmth, and humor, or at least charm, to offset the character's self-absorbed, rebellious nature. For Jonathan and me, Maureen represented a real stylistic and vocal challenge. We saw and heard a lot of women who all sounded similar. The typical young female sound in the musical theater of the eighties and early nineties was a slightly more nasal high belt or bright mix that was a byproduct of the Andrew Lloyd Webber shows, including *Cats, Song and Dance, Starlight Express,* and *Evita,* William Finn's *Falsettoland,* and British imports like *Les Misérables, Miss Saigon,* and *Blood Brothers.* I understood. The high, almost piercing sound was dramatic and in a lot of cases effective. But to my ears, that sound was soulless. It sounded like an onslaught. I didn't feel as if I was being sung *to.* More like I was being sung *at.*

So you can imagine the thrill (and relief) Jonathan and I felt when a young woman named Idina Menzel came in. She sang "Something to Talk About" from Bonnie Raitt's multiplatinum album *Luck of the Draw.* It was the new hot pop song for women to audition with, so I had heard a lot of it over the previous couple of years, but when Idina sang it, what came out were her warmth, earthiness, groove, and her blue-eyed soul sound. Think Dusty Springfield, Annie Lennox, Bonnie Raitt, or even as far back as Lulu singing "To Sir with Love." As if that weren't enough, Idina followed up with "When a Man Loves a Woman," the R & B classic made famous by Percy Sledge. It was a slow, soulful 6/8 classic R & B ballad that she killed. Jonathan and I were ready to cast her from the first phrase she sang. She didn't sound like anyone else, and she had great time and brought elite musicianship.

Michael still had to do what he had to do, putting her through her acting paces. Thankfully, though she had no previous theater experience, Idina succeeded. That meant casting her was a no-brainer. What a much-needed breath of fresh air Idina was, and what a find by Bernie. Jonathan was thrilled, and I let out a deep exhale.

The complete opposite happened as we brought in women to audition for the role of Joanne. No problem finding someone who could sing. We saw and heard a parade of great young Black female singers, one after the other. An embarrassment of riches. I really enjoyed those auditions, because it was a lot of Aretha Franklin, Chaka Khan, and Etta James, with a side of Gloria Gaynor. Yet Jonathan didn't respond to any of them, as good as most of them were. Then a young woman named Fredi Walker came in. She sang "Joy to the World," the Hoyt Axton song made popular by Three Dog Night, and when she left, Jonathan turned to everyone and said triumphantly, "That's my Joanne!" (It was the same reaction he'd had after Anthony Rapp's audition in 1994 when he'd announced, "That's Mark!") What else was there to say? It was still curious to me that when all of them except Jonathan had said after Daphne auditioned, "That's Mimi!" Jonathan hadn't. Yet here he was so sure that Fredi was Joanne. It's not that Fredi wasn't worthy, but we'd seen a lot of good Joanne candidates during the audition process—and Shelley Dickinson, who had played the role in 1994, was also great. The only thing I knew was that this was something I could never know, the thing that's in the writer's mind only: how they imagine their characters. For Jonathan, Fredi was the perfect realization of Joanne.

Wilson Jermaine Heredia came in to audition for the role of Angel. Up to that point we'd had no luck whatsoever finding, much less casting, someone who would fit the role as Jonathan and Michael had imagined it. We needed a tenor who could sing a vocally challenging role and handle its physical and dance requirements, all of which was going to add up to a strenuous and taxing role to play eight shows a week. I had ideas from the 1994 production of things that I was hoping to change for Angel in the next version, which would add a little more vocal stress on whoever had to sing the part. When Wilson sauntered in, it was clear he was a lovely young man, effortlessly cheery, but as was true for many others who had auditioned for both productions, the theater experience was new to him and he hadn't prepared any material. I asked him what songs he knew, and to my great delight, he said, "I know Stevie Wonder."

"Do you know 'I Wish'?" I asked.

He did, so we sang it in a few keys. I did more vocal exercises than usual with him to check out his range and try to expand it, to see what his voice might be capable of. To me he sounded a bit like the neo-soul singer Terence Trent D'Arby, whom I loved. Wilson passed my obstacle course with flying colors. Michael, Jim, and Jonathan all liked him too. He had an openness and a sunny disposition. He was incredibly likable and, like Daphne, who was of Panamanian ancestry, Wilson, of Dominican ancestry, had an easy Latin swag about him. The fact that he didn't have experience in the theater didn't matter. We were all in the business of meeting them where they were, guiding and teaching as we went.

At last we were getting down to the wire, within shouting distance of our first rehearsal, but we still didn't have a Collins or Roger. Collins, I had learned from Jonathan's lyrics in 1994, was a college professor—one I imagined to be a counterculture genius—and an activist and empath who probably rolled out of bed every morning and rolled up a fatty before he went to teach. For that role, Bernie had an ace up his sleeve, or so he thought. He had recently cast Jesse L. Martin in the play *I Ain't Yo' Uncle* at Hartford Stage, where he and Will had cast so many plays over the years. When we had made the decision early in 1995 that Collins didn't necessarily have to be a white person, Bernie thought of Jesse immediately. Then came the rub. Bernie had asked Jesse to come to New York on his day off to audition for *Rent*. Not once, but six times, and Jesse blew off all six. He told Bernie, "I don't want to do a musical." Okay. But not okay by Bernie, who said to Jesse, "This isn't a regular musical. You can just come in, hang out at the piano, and sing like you sing." So that autumn, after request number seven, Jesse came in and proved Bernie's hunch was dead-on. Jesse was great. He didn't prepare an audition song, so he and I made our way through "Amazing Grace" in a handful of keys. He was a cross between a classically trained actor and Marvin Gaye. He had a real presence about him, another incredibly handsome, charming, wise, and likable man. He was awesome in every way. After he left, there was a brief conversation among all of us, but it was unnecessary. It was obvious that if Jesse would agree to play the role, we would cast him immediately. Thankfully, he did.

Before we got on to casting Roger, we still hadn't cast one of the members of the community who would be featured as Gordon, a featured vocalist in the "Life Support" group who would play multiple other roles, among them a drug dealer and a homeless man. Jonathan asked a friend of his whom he knew from Naked Angels, another of the small, artistically vibrant downtown theaters, if he would audition. He came in, and although he was a little measured and sounded like he lacked confidence in his singing voice, which I thought sounded good, he brought a level of gravity to the room that I immediately latched on to. Maybe I assigned that quality to him since he was Jonathan's friend. Regardless, he was a lovely guy and the decision to cast him was an easy one. We only learned after he left the room that the man, who'd introduced himself by his nickname, Toby, was Timothy Britten Parker, the brother of Sarah Jessica Parker. I got it. He was from a show business family, hence the comfort and ease he brought to his audition, his vocal shyness notwithstanding. I knew I could help him sing more confidently if necessary, but it wasn't. After we cast him and got into rehearsals, he was fine.

Now we were at the end of the line, with a week or so to cast Roger. Even though Tony Hoylen, who had done the previous version, had a cool-sounding voice, Michael was seeking to upgrade the role in ways that only he knew. Michael needed to cast a love interest for Mimi, and the character had to be believable as a young, up-and-coming rock star. He needed to have the "it" factor. Jonathan and I were looking for a stronger singer, and I had been looking overall for a significant vocal upgrade in this new cast. I wanted a group with both feet firmly planted in the world of rock, pop, and R & B. And so far, so good. We were hoping and praying that there was someone still out there, knowing that Bernie, Will, and David had been working creatively and furiously for months trying to find someone who could play the role.

For decades *The Village Voice* was New York's (and probably the nation's) most progressive weekly newspaper. *The Voice*, as it was lovingly called, launched in the mid-fifties and had its heyday in the countercultural sixties. For me the great thing about it was that it would run extensive articles, editorials, and reviews of all the artistic happenings in the city. There was info about music, theater, visual arts, and all the known and not so well known venues where one could find them. Toward the back of each weekly edition the paper ran an extensive classifieds section for the arts: advertisements from painters and sculptors looking for assistants and models, strippers looking for costume designers (they needed *something* to strip off), and bands looking for musicians. Bernie's associate, David, had a brilliant idea. Since Roger was an up-and-coming rock star and heartthrob, he *had* to play guitar, so David scoured the classified ads for guitar teachers, which were not in short supply. He called everyone who had put an ad in *The Voice* and asked if they had students who were rock singers and could play well. What a brilliant idea! If they did, David told them to have the students come to his casting office on Friday from 3:00 to 5:00 p.m. and they could audition for the role of Roger for a new off-Broadway musical. All that was required was that they bring in a song they could sing and play.

That Friday at three, David went into Bernie's office. "How many do we have?" Bernie asked.

"Well," David replied, "we have seventeen guys who all look like Alice Cooper, and one handsome blond guy who's kind of normal-looking." All of them auditioned, and the blond guy really knocked Bernie out. He performed U2's "Red Hill Mining Town," from their groundbreaking album *The Joshua Tree*. And he was a solid guitar player to boot. There was only one problem: he couldn't, or for whatever reason just didn't, sing with his eyes open. Bernie didn't care. Not his problem. He called Jim at the end of the day and said, "I got one!"

The following day the rest of us met the kind-of-normal-looking handsome blond guy. His name was Adam Pascal, and he showed up in a black leather jacket, guitar in tow. While talking with Adam, we found out that he had actually heard about the audition through his childhood friend Idina Menzel, whom we had just cast as Maureen, not the guitar teachers. Adam and Idina had been neighbors in Syosset, Long Island. As he had done the previous Friday at Bernie's office, he sang and played great, bringing elite musicianship to the proceedings just as Idina had. *Must be something in the water in Syosset*, I thought. After he left, we discussed how well he sang and how good-looking he was—a perfect package except for the eyes-closed-while-he-was-singing thing. For his callback we gave him a couple of songs from the show, one of which was "Your Eyes," a song Jonathan had written for Roger to sing to Mimi as she lay on a table, weak and barely holding on to life. For this it seemed he would *have* to make eye contact with her. But again his eyes were mostly closed. After Adam left, Michael said to Bernie, "Just tell him the only thing he needs to think about and do is sing with his eyes open." If Adam could accomplish that, Michael would take it from there.

On the last day Adam came in, there were two rows of chairs behind the audition tables, which stretched about twelve feet long. There were a lot of people from the Workshop there that day, including Jim and Martha. Bernie was there, as were Kevin and Jeffrey and the creative team. As concerned, hopeful, and nervous as we all were (it seemed to us that it was Adam or no one), the person who was sweating the most bullets was Bernie. He was so good at what he did and made his job look so easy that I was somewhat shocked to see that he was the most anxious. But I understood why. His company was called Bernie Telsey Casting.

I thought back to Daphne's 1994 callback. My hope was that Adam would have the same story, that he went home, prepared, and now would come in, nail the audition, and make our decision an easy one. To our immense relief, to put it mildly, Adam's third audition was indeed the charm. He sang to Bernie, who played the role of Mimi, with his eyes open, and we cast him as Roger. It turned out that he didn't have some sort of nervous tic or similar problem causing him to close his eyes. Instead, it was probably the result of a long-standing habit. Having played in a lot of bands in a lot of venues, I knew that many of us sang with our eyes closed just because of the lighting. It was bright, close, and disarming in some of those small, loud rock clubs. I thought maybe that was the reason. In any case, we were done with auditions!

Well, nearly done.

We still hadn't found the woman who would be the featured singer in "Seasons of Love," as well as other featured roles in the homeless community. We had auditioned a lot of women, but no one had a voice that Jonathan and I liked (even among the Joanne women) or the gravitas that Michael wanted. We wouldn't find her until rehearsal had begun. But at that moment, we had basically found the cast of the 1995–96 production. It had been a gratifying seven months ultimately. Sure, Bernie was frustrated and anxious early and often, but it turned out to be a fantastic collaboration, with all of us on the creative side finding out more about each other's tastes and Bernie, Will, and David looking under every possible rock to meet all our hopes. And they did it! They achieved what was seemingly impossible. They found a cast that accurately reflected Jonathan, Michael, and Jim's vision of the East Village: a group of smart, shrewd, and highly skilled musical actors, singers, and dancers. We would begin rehearsal in a month or so.

The other big thing that happened was that I found an apartment on West Fifty-Fifth Street, between Eighth and Ninth Avenues. I was finally off Lonny's couch and in my own crib, even if I still kept most of my stuff in storage because the apartment was only twelve by fourteen feet, plus a half kitchen and bathroom. There was room for a foam mattress and a small wooden table that I had built in my high school shop class. It was well made and well-traveled, having been with me through college and my first fifteen years in New York. I had written a boatload of music on that table over many years.

To say my building was the eyesore of a decent block would be to glorify it. It was a filthy, unkempt structure that flat out *reeked*, replete with cockroaches and, I imagined, not up to a single one of the city's codes. The building and all the apartments I saw in it were nasty. I knew there were lots of people living in less comfortable apartments all around New York, but I hadn't lived like that since my college days in Boston. (In those days it was the entire rodent family: roaches, mice, and rats. We bought a pet ferret to keep them away.) This apartment wasn't dangerous or anything, because of the block it was on; it was just disgusting. Its only saving grace was a small patch of green outside my one tiny window. Staring out at it gave me a tiny shred of peace. The one great piece of wisdom I picked up from a friend, after telling her about my out-of-control cockroach situation, was to go to Central Park and pick up some Osage oranges that fell from the trees and shrubs. They weren't orange, more yellowish green, and were part of the mulberry family. Their odor, she told me, was a natural repellent to cockroaches. So off I went every few weeks until winter to gather them off the ground. It worked!

Despite the roaches, I was happy to finally be in my own "home." It meant that I had a place I could come to at the end of a long day or night. And that brought a sense of stability. As the subbing and club date gigs started to pick up again, and as *Rent* rehearsals neared, I found comfort knowing that I wouldn't be there very much, because even though it was my own place, it was still a dump.

Jesse, Fredi, Idina, Daphne, and Adam in rehearsal at the New York Theatre Workshop, 1995.

REHEARSAL
December 1995

OUR FIRST REHEARSAL was more of a prerehearsal rehearsal, a truncated music session with Jonathan, Michael, the cast, and me at NYTW's Forty-First Street space, where they still had offices, since their downtown location was currently occupied. There was just enough room for all of us and a piano. It was tight, but fine. Our first formal rehearsal at the Workshop wasn't scheduled until the following Tuesday, but Michael and Jonathan were eager to get the cast together so everyone could meet and we could sing. We assembled there for a 1:00 p.m. start. I could rehearse for only two hours because I had to play a club date in Albany later that day. It was a three-hour drive from the city, so I had brought along my tuxedo and dress shoes in a hanging bag and my pedals and cables in a separate case. When Idina arrived, she too had a hanging bag with formalwear and an accessory bag because she also had a club date that night, only she would have to drive up to Boston. We bonded a little bit over the club date culture, which she knew well, and I always felt a special kinship with her because of that.

Starting with the 1994 production, Michael and I had developed a routine. Since we didn't rehearse the songs in order,

Michael gave everyone some context for each song, talking a bit about the lyrics and whatever else he needed to communicate. After he was done explaining that to the cast, I would begin rehearsal by leading a vocal warmup for them. Every musical director had their own. Mine had a bit of everything: long held notes (good for the breathing), scales, arpeggios, unison, harmony, rhythmic stuff, tongue twisters for consonants, and a little Stevie Wonder at the end. These exercises gave me my first listen to the overall group sound we had assembled one by one through the audition period. They sounded great and were mentally on their toes, easily picking up everything I threw at them. Even though it was just a warmup, I was pleased at how effortlessly their voices blended and how musical everyone was. Everyone had great pitch and time. It was reassuring to my ears. When I glanced at Jonathan, though he had a bit of a poker face, I knew he heard it too.

After we finished I said to the group, "Okay everyone, you ready? Let's carve," and we began learning "Seasons of Love," though without our featured female soloist. The company still had to learn the song, so we'd be fine until she joined us. I had added some "oohs" to the second verse since the 1994 version, and they sounded good. I caught Jonathan nodding his approval out of the corner of my eye, even though we hadn't spoken about it previously. An hour or so later, we were done, and it sounded even better than I had anticipated. The cast heard it too. It was a great song written by a great songwriter and already sung beautifully by this group. Making music together creates bonds. In case some of the cast members didn't know that already, they sure knew it after we had finished. Everyone felt the warm, satisfying feeling in the music and the air. In that cramped space, something magical was underway.

The following Tuesday at 10:00 a.m., we congregated at the Workshop for the official start of rehearsals. We began as most new productions do, with a meet-and-greet for the cast, Jim and

MAKING RENT

the entire NYTW staff, the crew, and the creative team: Jonathan, Michael, and me; our choreographer, Marlies Yearby; costume designer, Angela Wendt; set designer, Paul Clay; lighting designer, Blake Burba; and sound designer, Kurt Fischer. We met our stage manager, Crystal Huntington, who would guide us through rehearsals, as well as Kathy Haley, our assistant stage manager. We also met the Workshop's publicity and box office staff and everyone else who helped steer the ship and make it run. This included the wonderful folks I had met when we did the 1994 production—Martha Banta, Linda Chapman, Kate Broderick, and production manager Sue White, who did so much more than her job title suggested.

After a short break, featuring bagels, coffee, and juice, we continued the work we had begun uptown. We did a warmup followed by a review of "Seasons of Love." Happily, most of the cast had done their homework. More than a handful of them had already memorized the song, and reviewing the harmonies went more smoothly than I had expected. Even after only two hours together the previous Saturday, everyone was singing with more self-assuredness, and they were exhibiting a mainstay of being a musician: listening to each other. No one was trying to out-sing anyone else. No one was trying to stand out. They were just being themselves, together. It was cool hearing that. The next song we would rehearse, logically, would be "Seasons of Love B," which was similar to the "A" version, but with different vocal assignments because it came later in act two, under different dramatic circumstances. I asked Jonathan if I could remove a harmony he had written, because we didn't have the personnel to support it. In addition to that, there would still be a two-, then a three-part harmony to come in that short reprise, so I thought the build would be smoother without it. Without hesitation he said, "Sure. Go ahead." He trusted me in front of everyone. I believed that sent a message to the cast. "You can trust this guy. I do." We never spoke about that moment, but I was grateful it happened.

Next we started working on the title song, "Rent." We dealt with the end of the song, which is the part where the whole community comes together, first in two groups (a group of seven, followed by a group of eight), then all of them together. Jonathan knew he didn't want any harmony in the beginning of that section (he indicated to me where the harmonies should start), but rather than having them sing an octave apart, men on the bottom and women on top, I asked the men and women to sing in unison on the same pitch. Much to my surprise, honestly, it produced a stronger dramatic effect. *Hmm, blind squirrel finds acorn,* I thought. It was a more robust, dramatic, in-your-face sound and the lyrics were easier to understand. Then something happened for me that represented a kind of sea change in how I would continue those music rehearsals. After hearing the first thirty-two bars I had taught, Jonathan came up to me and said quietly, "I have to go do a few things. I know you'll take care of the rest of it."

Even though Jonathan and I had built up a degree of trust during the year we had known each other, that reassurance was, as I took it, his endorsement of my understanding of his writing. I think he knew that I would be able to elevate his work going forward in a way that he would be comfortable with. All I said was "Sure, happy to do it." But mentally and physically that was another moment where I exhaled. I was sure that Jonathan and I were on the same page, and he and I both knew he could trust me. Even though I had done plenty of vocal arranging for other shows, *Rent* felt different. Maybe it was because I respected Jonathan so much as a songwriter. He was just plain better and more original than any of the other composers I had worked with. In that moment I continued my work with the fresh stamp of Jonathan's approval, which manifested in my feeling freer to experiment and maybe even fail a time or two. That brief exchange helped me become a more creative and thoughtful vocal arranger.

We eventually finished "Rent," and then through the day we hit more of the full-cast songs: "Will I?" "Finale B," then, after letting Wilson go to work on some Angel choreography with Marlies, the "I'll Cover You" reprise. Jesse just sat and listened, took it all in, and heard what would be surrounding him vocally. There was still the missing element of our female "Seasons of Love" soloist, still not cast, who I hoped would eventually figure into this song prominently, one of the mental notes I kept in my head from the previous production. Nevertheless, we did get through the song and finished the day with a couple of the smaller group numbers—"Santa Fe" and some of the songs featuring our homeless community. After that first long day was over, I was inspired and exhausted. It had been a day rich in playing, creating, and imagining what could be. The following day would be mentally taxing for the cast, as we would be learning "Christmas Bells" and "La Vie Boheme," songs that were very complicated, sung by the entire company, episodic in nature, and *long*. Almost everyone had never heard those songs, so *bring your patience with your recording devices everyone*, I thought. For the creative team, however, our day wasn't finished with the end of rehearsal.

After the cast had all left shortly after 6:00 p.m., some tables were set up in the middle of the room, just as we had done for our auditions the previous months. Once again, as if in flashback, there we all were: Jonathan, Michael, and me beside Jim, Martha, and Bernie, and now Marlies as well. I had two seats: the seat behind the table and my seat at the piano. Bernie brought in a lovely young woman named Gwen Stewart to audition for, among other ensemble roles, our "Seasons of Love" soloist. She was poised, showing no signs of being overwhelmed by the moment. She had two Broadway shows under her belt—*Truly Blessed* and *Starmites*. Introductions were made, and she and I met at the piano. She hadn't brought in any music, so we talked about what songs we both knew. Maybe we would have found a song or two, but she was intent on singing a church song. She asked me if I knew "He Looked Beyond My Faults." I didn't. My church repertoire was limited to a dozen or so songs, and that wasn't one of them. I learned later that it was a well-known, well-worn part of the church canon. Kind of thought of as the other "Amazing Grace." She sang the song a cappella, and it was beautiful—soulful, honest, and musical, all of my favorite qualities. I asked Gwen about her training and she told us that she'd never studied music and didn't read it, that her voice was a gift from God that she never questioned. Sensing the faith-based part of her life, Michael asked, "One of the characters you'd be playing curses in the show. Are you okay with that?"

"That's the character who's swearing. It's not me," she replied. I learned a couple qualities about Gwen from that answer: her ability to compartmentalize and her openness to whatever was happening. Her response was an objective, practical response to Michael's question and I loved it. I wasn't the least bit concerned that she didn't read music. More than half the cast didn't read music. I wasn't there to judge them on their musical training. A lot of them hadn't studied formally, so the approach that seemed to me the most logical way to deal with written music was something I had done for years. When I first met a cast, I would ask three questions to be answered by a show of hands. One: who could read music? Two: who knew that when the dots went up, it meant for their voices to go higher, and when the dots went down, it meant for their voices to go lower? And three: who had absolutely no clue what was in front of them, other than the lyrics? In my experience, the most hands went up for number two. Rhythm and rests could easily be taught by repetition and plain old counting, as well as listening to vocal cues from others as a guide to when someone should come in with their part. If it wasn't a solo, the person could sing and interact with the others musically, using their listening skills and innate musicality to get the job done. It wasn't rocket science. It was communication, and the language was melody and harmony. Just like *Rent* itself, a play whose language was melody and harmony.

After Gwen was gone, I exclaimed, "I've never heard *anyone* sing like her!" Her sound was so one-in-a-million to me. Not the range (although I would be surprised by that a couple of days later) but her tone, timbre, and print. Happily, everyone else in the room loved her too, so Bernie made the call, Gwen accepted the offer, and she became a part of the *Rent* cast starting that Wednesday morning.

The following day began with reviewing Tuesday's work and introducing Gwen to everyone. I had talked to Gwen prior to rehearsal and reminded her to keep her cassette recorder on and catch whatever she could. We'd fill in the rest in a day or two. Not to worry. Michael and I had already blocked out time for Gwen and me, so my hope was to start working on "Seasons of Love" and fill in all her other parts along the way. As musical as Gwen was, along with her great ear, she was fairly relaxed about getting caught up. After the music review with the company, we started carving into "Christmas Bells." Like I remembered from the previous year, that song contained a lot of information sung by a lot of people, and eventually all that information was sung simultaneously. The end of the number was intentionally cacophonous, representing the sound of the East Village during the holiday season, and as far as I was concerned it was fine that our audience wouldn't hear everything perfectly the first time. The entire song was episodic, like a film. Michael knew who was who in this new fifteen-person version and where and when they would be singing. That song featured everyone in a variety of situations and roles—street vendors, cops, junkies, and the homeless—and it contained fast-moving solos, duets, trios, quartets, and quintets, a wide spectrum of musical options. Teaching that song to the full cast took the entire morning, but they did well. Of course they did.

That afternoon we dug into "La Vie Boheme." Again there were a lot of solos, duets, trios, and quartets, and larger group vocals as the song built. In short, every permutation you could imagine. It was truly a masterful composition by Jonathan, and a great "list" song to boot—think Cole Porter's "You're the Top" or Sondheim's "A Little Priest," songs that elaborate on a theme with a series of examples that build to an emotionally resonant conclusion. The lists in "La Vie Boheme" were better than most, and the song brought much more than that: dramatic exposition, conflict, intimacy, romance, and, ultimately, celebration, all wrapped up in one remarkable musical package. Jonathan's act-one finale was already a tour de force in the craft of songwriting, and he had reconceived and rewritten parts of it after the 1994 production. Man, what a day that was. Exhausting and thrilling for all. For me it was mentally draining due to the level of concentration I had to maintain, and by the end of that day's rehearsal even my hair hurt.

After everyone had left, Gwen and I had a few minutes to get her up to speed. We started with "Seasons of Love." She learned her eight-bar solo in the second verse, and we dug into the final chorus. "We're looking for some kind of call-and-response thing here," I said. "Whatever you're hearing would be a great place for us to start." The next day Michael blocked out a little more time for the two of us. Gwen came in with a five-by-seven note card with some sentences scribbled on the front and back and said, "I've written some lyrics for the end of the song." She showed them to me and asked, "Do you like them?" I did. I thought they were personal, meaningful, and remarkably appropriate, especially considering that she had first heard "Seasons of Love" only two days earlier. Pretty darn intuitive, and in addition to writing the lyrics she had composed a melody for them. All I had said to her previously was that the very end of the song needed to lift the last chorus even higher, to help the song build to a climax. She did all that and more, with the lyrics:

> You've got to remember the love
> You know that love is a gift from up above.
> Share love, give love, spread love.
> Measure, measure your life in love.

She helped complete the song with a long, almost operatic (or, more accurately, "gospelatic") high C at the end on the lyric "love." She held the note for about six beats, riffed *higher*, then finished the riff by snaking her way downward. In one breath! She repeated "measure your life in love," which was a reaffirmation and would intermingle with and finish alongside her castmates. Gwen had written the end of "Seasons of Love." Neither Jonathan nor I had written anything down, and I didn't contribute anything beyond the general musical idea of the last chorus and the descant. It was all Gwen. Her understanding of the song, pouring her faith into it, and sealing the message of what Jonathan had written were incredible and dramatically spot-on. Jonathan, Michael, the cast, and I were truly blessed by what she had brought to the song that would open act two. It was soulful, exciting, and beautiful—all very Gwen Stewart.

The next step was adding Gwen into the "I'll Cover You" reprise. Not only was the reprise, as we referred to it, Angel's memorial, but it was also a reflection of what had been happening in New York since the early eighties and into the nineties. There were so many memorials like the one Jonathan wrote in *Rent*, and I played a handful of them during my time. AIDS tore through the artistic community, so whether one was a singer or musician, there was always a memorial to attend or to sing or play for. As for the reprise, I wanted to add a trio to help lift the song—and hopefully Jesse—and add another layer as we made our way to the chorus. Since Gwen had established herself in "Seasons of

Love," we wanted to bring her back for this section. Jonathan had already put in the lyric "with a thousand sweet kisses I'll cover you" from the act-one "I'll Cover You" in 1994. I built upon that for this version by adding in Byron on a lower harmony and then Fredi on a third part. So now we had a call-and-response between Jesse and Gwen, then between Jesse, Gwen, and Byron, then between all four of them. All while the rest of the cast was holding down the fort, singing "525,600 minutes, 525,000 moments so dear," which Jonathan had put into the song. The cherry on top was that in the chorus ("Oh lover, I'll cover you") I had Gwen and Jessie in two-part harmony, singing "Yeah, yeah, yeah, yeah," just as Collins and Angel had done in act one. It all came together very soulfully and authentically, and Jonathan and Michael approved.

The next step was to start doing the smaller stuff, so our named characters could start to build their relationships through song. Michael was big on having whoever was learning a new song sing to each other, no matter their unfamiliarity with the material. It was all about relating to each other from the jump. We began with nine members of our community in "Life Support." Their names for that scene were Paul (the support group leader), Steve, Gordon, Ali, Pam, and Sue, in addition to Angel, Collins, and Mark. "Life Support" was based on Friends In Deed, a well-known counseling center that formed in 1991, as the scourge of HIV/AIDS was ravaging the New York community. It was founded by Cynthia "Cy" O'Neal, with the help of her friend, the iconic director Mike Nichols, as a space where HIV-positive people could come and talk about their condition, fears, and whatever they were experiencing as a byproduct of their diagnosis, which was for many a death sentence. Organically, Friends In Deed expanded to include the caregivers, most often partners and families, who were grieving in their own ways.

Jonathan had volunteered there and attended meetings as he watched his friends Gordon, Ali, and Pam each succumb to the disease. The mission for Friends In Deed was acutely present as the "Life Support" song unfolded.

> There's only us. There's only this.
> Forget regret, or life is yours to miss.
> No other road, no other way.
> No day but today.

A beautiful tribute by Jonathan to his late friends, in the best way he knew.

Throughout the latter half of 1995 and into January 1996, Jonathan wrote furiously. He finally knew the characters and the people who would be inhabiting them, plus the sound of the band he was writing for. As I saw it, his uncanny songwriting ability was the not-so-secret sauce and was probably aided by the help of his ongoing dramaturgical work with Lynn and Michael. In noticeable ways he started writing for the specific actors of our newest cast. Once he knew we would be casting Taye, Jonathan wrote the song "You'll See" specifically for Taye's vocal range and the energy he brought to the character: his smooth-as-honey manner, which was a part of Taye's overall vibe. Taye's diction was great, which was absolutely necessary to communicate the plotlines the song set in motion. Aside from the exposition in "You'll See," the song establishes Benny as a complex character who, though seen as the villain by the others, truly believes in what he's doing and genuinely wants his friends to be a part of it. The audience would have a lot of information to digest in a relatively short song, and Taye could deliver.

Jonathan was extremely keen and observant and, like his idol Stephen Sondheim, a rabid notetaker. We had enough proof to know he was a smart, resourceful, and gifted lyricist. He rewrote Roger's first solo, "One Song Glory," over the very same melody and accompaniment that he used for "Right Brain" from the 1994 production, leaning into the lyrical specificity of Roger's abyss into which he was staring. I thought his most inspired artistry and craftsmanship came together in "What You Own," a duet for Roger and Mark late in act two. He had combined two songs from 1994, "Real Estate," sung by Mark, and "Open Road," sung by Roger, one a country-western song and the other a wistful ballad—into an alt-rock masterpiece. I thought that the new duet was absolutely superb songwriting, and it seemed tailored specifically to Adam and Anthony's voices. When I first heard "What You Own," I was so grateful to have done the 1994 production, so I could see and hear how Jonathan merged two songs and two characters' dire circumstances into one astounding song. It had the feel and power, both musically and lyrically, of a true eleven-o'clock number, where two of his main characters confront and decide to act on the emotional crossroads in front of them, all of which I found jaw-dropping.

Jonathan had solved almost the entire puzzle of his musical by the time we began rehearsals in December. Each song was better than the one—or two—it replaced, but most importantly, the entire show had a timeline that could be easily followed. That was important, because the songs were so lyrically dense as they came tumbling out, one after another, that audiences would have been easily confused without some guidance. It was now abundantly clear that the show took place over the course of a single year, the seasons marked by lyrics and spoken words, which was one less thing for the audience to try to figure out. That was Jonathan's second biggest accomplishment. His biggest was that from 1995 to early January 1996, everything (except one, just *one* song) he brought in was dead on the money. Not a clunker to be found. However you wanted to put it, he was in the zone, in the garden spot, the mayor's office, and he was *burnin*'! I'd never seen or heard such prodigious writing in my life. Even though I was never near any part of the Sondheim orbit, Jonathan's output was the closest to those legendary stories we had all read and heard about. The huge block of work that Jonathan created during that time was mind-blowing.

Everything was going well, but not all was perfect and harmonious. There was a little infighting among our creative staff. Between Jonathan and me, between Jonathan and Lynn pushing back on Michael's thoughts and wishes, and between the actors, myself, Michael, and Jonathan. It manifested itself in a few significant ways. When I started teaching Jesse the "I'll Cover You" reprise, the plan was to build it on him, deploying his musical strengths and his acting skill to make the song ascend appropriately and comfortably for Jesse the singer as well as Collins the character. It was an approach that Michael and I had agreed upon back in 1994. We would custom-tailor some of the songs, where there was wiggle room, to suit the strengths of the actors, musically or otherwise.

In the case of the reprise I knew that I wanted the song to be a long, slow vocal build from beginning to end. Michael suggested that Jesse and I work patiently and methodically at the piano, and so we began. After a while though, Jonathan got a little antsy. He said, essentially, why don't you just do this? Or that? He wasn't into the careful, more granular way that Michael, Jesse, and I were approaching the song. Michael tried to make Jonathan understand what we were doing and why we were doing it. But at a certain point, Jonathan's impatience ruled, and he said he wanted Jesse to sing it the way Pat Briggs had done in the 1994 version. Michael countered, in the nicest way, "Well, Jesse is Jesse. He sings the way he sings. That's one of the reasons we cast him." We wanted to build the performance with Jesse, so he had his own musical stake in it, and Michael would help guide the song wherever it went, all while keeping Jonathan's melody at its core. Jesse was an exceptional actor, so we knew his version of the song would be all truth and no pretense. It was a little touchy there for a while, and it was the first whiff of conflict between Jonathan and me since we had met. In the end I had to choose sides, and loyal as I was to Jonathan, I sided with Michael and Jesse and trusted my own musical knowledge and instincts. We got through it, but it was sticky.

The upside of that experience was that when it came time to create a melody for Wilson to sing in "Contact," it was a less bumpy teaching experience. Here, Jonathan hadn't written anything that he was married to, and I think he understood more fully that we would do the same thing with Wilson as we had done with Jesse, only with fewer melodic guardrails. Jonathan did provide a basic four-bar melody, and he knew he wanted to include the new lyric, "take me," as well as "today for me, tomorrow for you" from Angel's song in act one.

As for deciding what parts of Wilson's vocal range to explore, Michael's ear-opening note to me was, "Remember that he's as much a young man as he is a girly girl." We experimented, Wilson and I, with the lower part of his register at the beginning of the vocal, and when the guitar solo began on the prerecorded track, we shot the vocal into his falsetto to communicate that he was of two creatures. We settled back into his stronger tenor, a bit more androgynous-sounding (hello, Terence Trent D'Arby), and then at the very end we got him up into his falsetto again, with his voice going higher and higher, finishing his vocal to represent Angel finishing his time on earth and shooting like a star into the heavens. It was all a dream sequence, obviously, but a dream that was conceivable as he lay sleeping, sick and dying from his illness, unable to withstand the pain of his earthly existence, all set to the musical tapestry of the dance clubs—the late-night rave havens of techno, house, and electronica. One could easily envision a young man like Angel, as seen or as clandestine as he chose, at Limelight, one of New York's premiere dance clubs during the eighties and nineties. All this to say that it wasn't a reach to believe that the Club Kid nightspots were the places Angel felt safety, comfort, freedom, and peace, where he felt he could be his truest self.

Then came "Without You." As Jonathan had written it, it was a solo for Mimi. Daphne had sung it beautifully in the 1994 version, or so I thought. Apparently it still wasn't beautiful or satisfying enough for Jonathan. *Oh my god, here we go again*, I realized, when this started to become clear. It was absolutely Jonathan's right to go through every combination of who would sing a song he still felt unsure about. Out of respect and as a courtesy to him, Michael and I tried out the song on everyone. What none of us knew was that in his mind Michael had already built the storytelling and staging that would accompany the song. After assigning the song to multiple combinations of other characters and working on it for parts of three days, Jonathan finally agreed to give it back to Mimi, as he had originally intended, and I added Roger into the last verses and coda. Not only did that drop a little much-needed harmony into the song, but Adam's vocal strength helped Daphne push a little more air into the end, and they sounded great, putting all the emotional muscle they could conjure at that point in the show, when their characters had both become very weak. Because of Michael's elegant staging, when they sang the last "you" together at Roger's bedside, it was emotionally packed, as if they'd sung "I'd give my last breath on earth for you."

We had begun that week's rehearsal on Tuesday, December 19, and rehearsed until the Saturday before Christmas. During the short Christmas break, Jonathan's parents, who had retired to Albuquerque, New Mexico, wanted Jonny, as they called him, to come for a quick visit. Jonathan told me he didn't really want to go—his mind was on the show—but that he'd feel guilty if he didn't. A little added incentive for him to go was that his sister, Julie, and her two young sons, whom he absolutely adored, would be there. When he got back to New York a few days later, he told me he was glad he'd made the trip. He hadn't seen his parents for a long time and he wouldn't see them again until the show opened. After the brief holiday respite, we continued in earnest through a memorable early January, when the tension ramped up (again) from all sides.

The last, at least for the time being, big songwriting task ahead of Jonathan was to rewrite the song he had written earlier that year, the one everyone heard and no one liked, titled "Love of My Life," for Maureen and Joanne. I remember going to Jonathan's apartment in December and on his wall near the piano was a series of sticky notes, each with a song title written on it and all placed in the order they came in the show. It was a musical version of storyboarding, a technique used in filmmaking. Where "Love of My Life" used to be, the square yellow note read, "Maureen/Joanne boffo comedy song." I liked the word "boffo." Very old-school. Jonathan told me he realized that maybe such broad comedy wasn't the right way to go, but he still hadn't solved the lyrical puzzle. However, he did say to me that he had a clearer idea of the direction of the music now that he had heard Idina and Fredi sing.

In rehearsal, after we had gotten through the entire first pass of all the music we had, Michael started gently reminding, then less gently reminding, then not at all gently reminding Jonathan to write the new Maureen/Joanne song. If Jonathan was writing that song, it certainly wasn't in the daytime. During the hours of 10:00 a.m. to 6:00 p.m. he was in the rehearsal room, sitting in his chair, hiding behind the *New York Times*. He was there, but he wasn't there—but because he was the composer and lyricist, he was *there*. I knew he wanted to hear how his songs were being executed, what Michael was doing with his work, and how the actors were handling his material. That was his right. He was curious, not controlling. What he failed to understand was that his presence, instead of inspiring, started *inhibiting* the actors from doing their best work. They felt watched and examined, rather than safe and free to try something and fail, or just try anything. After a time Michael felt it as well, but as an experienced director, he was used to that dynamic.

Not so much for some of the younger and less experienced company of actors. One of them came to Michael at the end of a rehearsal in early January and said to him, "We're all so self-conscious with Jonathan sitting here every day. Could you ask him to stay away, maybe even if it's just for half of the day?" Michael said he would talk to Jonathan, and the next morning he kept his word. I got down to the Workshop early, as was my habit, and in the kitchen that was adjacent to the rehearsal room I saw Michael and Jonathan having a conversation. I assumed Michael was explaining the situation to him. As Michael would tell me before rehearsal started, everything went fine. Jonathan understood and agreed to stay away for a while. There was only one problem. "What?" Michael asked, a little annoyed that there was a condition. Jonathan said, "I finished the new Maureen/Joanne song, and I was going to bring it in and play it for you this afternoon." What could Michael say? I mean, he had been dogging Jonathan for some time, so he readjusted the afternoon schedule.

Two o'clock came and Michael, Jim, Marlies, Martha, Fredi, Idina, and I were in the rehearsal room. In walked Jonathan with a Digital Audio Tape (DAT) and his DAT player. He plugged it into the rehearsal room's great sound system and what came out of those speakers blew my mind. An R & B shuffle? Are you fucking kidding me? Yep, there it was, with a very Jonathan-like piano part at its core, and with lyrics and melodies that were tailor-made for Maureen and Joanne, with a clear lyrical nod to Puccini's song for Musetta in *La bohème* ("*Quando me'n v'o*" known as "Musetta's Waltz"):

LA BOHÈME
> When I walk alone down the street,
> people stop and stare at me
> and look at my whole beauty
> from head to feet.

RENT
> Every single day I walk down the street.
> I hear people say, "Baby's so sweet."
> Ever since puberty, everybody stares at me.
> Boys, girls, I can't help it, baby.

We listened to the demo, and when it was over we all clapped. Hearing that incredible song right out of the oven was one of those magical moments none of us would ever forget. Just as Jonathan's idol, Stephen Sondheim, wrote "Send in the Clowns" for Glynis Johns in *A Little Night Music,* Jonathan had written "Take Me or Leave Me" for Fredi and Idina.

Jonathan came prepared with sheet music for the song printed up, so we were able to start working on it right away. It was a bit wordy, so we had to take it slow for Fredi and Idina to put the melodies and lyrics together. I threw in some harmonies in the second bridge and the last chorus, and it was all coming together nicely. It fit those women like two pairs of long, custom-made satin gloves. As I now routinely did, I spoke to Jonathan about a change I wanted to try—a modulation, or key change, out of the bridge into the last chorus. He had written one in a way that telegraphed that we were about to change keys, which was a pretty well-worn, traditional way of musical theater writing. But since there was nothing old-fashioned or traditional about this song, I suggested to Jonathan, "Why don't we do a 'Man in the Mirror' key change instead?" Jonathan's expression told me he had no idea what I was talking about. "Man in the Mirror" was a song from Michael Jackson's 1987 album *Bad*. The song was a number one hit and had been a staple of radio play for years. Apparently Jonathan hadn't heard it, or if he had, the key change didn't register. I explained it, then played him the chorus that led into the new key. What was especially great in the Michael Jackson song was how the key change came right on the lyric "change": "If you wanna make the world a better place / take a look at yourself and make that *change*."

I suggested that we hit the downbeat of the last bar of the bridge, rest, and then hit the new key, *bang!*, right on the downbeat of the last chorus. Fredi and Idina heard it once and nailed it, of course. It gave the song an unexpected lift, musically and dramatically, just like the one in the MJ recording. And most importantly, Jonathan and Michael liked it too. That was the last new song that Jonathan wrote for the 1995–96 production, and it was worth the wait. Michael was still unsatisfied with the opening, but Jonathan seemed content to open with "Tune Up A" and "Tune Up B" for the time being. I figured Jonathan would get around to reworking the opening during previews.

The following Sunday it started to snow. And snow. And snow some more. By the time it ended on Monday night, January 8, the historic "Blizzard of '96" had dropped two to three feet of snow on the city, and with the high winds it produced snowdrifts up to eight feet. The entire borough of Manhattan was brought to a standstill. All roads were impassable. The instant paralysis of the city was eerie and quiet, and kinda cool. The snowplows slowly emerged on Monday, plowing the major thoroughfares and dumping some of the snow into the Hudson or East River. They had plowed the avenues that ran north–south and the main cross streets, but not much else by the time we began band rehearsals on January 9.

The *Rent* band members schlepped down to the Workshop,

hauling all their gear through the newly snow-covered mountain that was Manhattan. Kenny had electric and acoustic guitars, an amplifier, and the appropriate pedals and cables to negotiate. Dan, who was playing guitars and keyboards, the same (I had ordered one of his keyboards, and it had arrived at the Workshop before the snow, thankfully). Our bass player, Steph, who Jeff had tapped to join us, had cargo that was similar to Kenny's and Dan's: two electric basses (one fretted and one fretless), pedals, cables, a bass head, and a speaker cabinet. Jeff probably had the toughest job. He had to lug his entire drum setup: the actual drums themselves—kick, snares, and tom-toms—the high hat and various cymbals, and the stands and hardware required to assemble everything. As if that weren't enough, he also had his electronic drum setup, which he had used for the 1994 production. All in all, he had about a hundred and twenty pounds of drums and hardware, plus another twenty or so pounds of electronics and accessories. While everyone else was able to take a cab downtown, Jeff had so much to haul that he and his wife drove down from Upper Manhattan, scaling enormous snowdrifts just to get his gear to the car.

The street outside the Workshop was still unplowed, but when everyone arrived at the corner of Bowery and East Fourth Street, the nearest possible drop-off spot coming downtown, they were met by our ever-reliable production manager, Sue White, and her battalion of staff and interns to help the musicians get their gear to the theater. They had shoveled a walking path from 79 East Fourth westward to Bowery. No small feat. That gesture alone told the band how important they were to the show. Navigating from their apartments to the East Village through the post-blizzard terrain was a difficult task for everyone, and the incredible effort and professional hospitality by Sue and her crew were a welcome sight. That small army trundled to the theater, gear in tow, and the band got set up as I was finishing rehearsal with the cast.

MAKING RENT
(103)

I was, once again, in the familiar rehearsal situation, only now with the added luxury of a second keyboard/guitar player. I had learned how to physically set up the band from the previous production, so we positioned ourselves as we would be once we got onstage. The band was in a semicircle, facing me. I had the best seat in town, the whole band facing me in stereo. I was lucky to have the ideal listening position, since hearing what they were playing was my number one priority as conductor and bandleader. The conducting part wasn't difficult by modern musical theater standards. My sole responsibility was to keep the *Rent* locomotive moving forward smoothly: get everyone into the songs in the right tempos, and where I needed to get them from one place to the next within songs, I'd either conduct with my head or my hand, whichever was available. But here in rehearsal I had to know what they were playing so I would know where to fit in as a keyboardist. I still had the responsibility of playing Jonathan's piano parts note for note, but I knew where I could stretch out and be a little more creative than in the previous version, as well as within the new material Jonathan had written over the last year. Those were the songs that the band and I would be creating together, which I was, to put it mildly, eagerly anticipating.

We began from the top of the show, rehearsing in the same room we had the previous year, on the same level as the stage, two floors below where the cast rehearsed. From the first note, *the first note*, that band was remarkable. It was the same drill as in 1994, but I had become acutely aware of how the band *should* sound, both from having done the earlier version and from having rehearsed the new material with our current cast. As I had done previously, I told the band the general direction I thought a song should go, citing comps like Queen's "Bohemian Rhapsody" for our song "Christmas Bells" or Booker T. and the MG's "Green Onions" for our song "We're OK" (I actually said to the band, "Think Booker T. on crack"). Maybe I'd play a bit of the tune on piano and sing some of it, so they knew the tempo, style, and overall vibe each song was living in, but that was about it. Their instincts were razor-sharp due to their vast musical knowledge and individual expertise on their instruments. As any rhythm section-only bands did, we instinctively divided ourselves into subsections. Jeff and Steph, who were on drums and bass, would listen to each other and work together to form the band's unshakable foundation. On the songs with two guitars, Dan (playing rhythm guitar) and Kenny (playing lead) would listen to each other and figure out how to play in a complementary way. Having two or more guitars is a difficult balance in any band because you have two identical instruments vying for the same musical territory. Being the rhythm, or second, guitar comes with a specific set of challenges. On one level, a rhythm guitarist has to put ego aside and play in a less showy and glamorous but equally important supporting role. The ones who really prove themselves in that role are a rare group. Dan was one such player. As accomplished and multidimensional a musician as he was, he put that all aside for the greater whole of the *Rent* band.

The new songs that Jonathan had written were where the band found itself. Songs like "You'll See," "Tango: Maureen," "Happy New Year" A and B, "Take Me or Leave Me," and "What You Own" gave the five of us the opportunity to carve out the identity of each tune, and, in turn, our own. In "You'll See," I added an acoustic guitar part for Dan throughout, including a part in the bridge where nothing was written when we received that chart, so we added a Pat Metheny-esque strumming in that section. In "Tango: Maureen," rather than playing the drums as he would for a traditional tango, I asked Jeff to think of the groove as more of a New Orleans–style rhumba, providing a degree of funk. Inspired by that, Kenny dialed up a tremolo effect onto his guitar sound, giving us some funk on funk. When Jonathan heard

Kenny's tremolo, he let out a little chuckle. He loved it. In "Santa Fe," I asked Kenny to put in a lot of bluesy acoustic guitar fills around Collins's vocal, which gave the song a rural, West Texas vibe. And with "One Song Glory" and "Happy New Year," we used a combination of electric and acoustic guitars (Kenny on electric, Dan on acoustic) to keep the songs rocking, but at a level below the full-on electric songs "Rent," "Out Tonight," and "What You Own." Most of the songs were partially fleshed out when we got them, but there were still gaps to fill, just as we had in 1994, resulting in more creative input by the band. It was a group effort, and I would listen as everyone came up with parts based on my suggestions or their taste or, most often, a combination of the two. There were the rare occasions where, since I knew what was going on dramaturgically from being in rehearsal, I would sing a part to Kenny or sing a drum fill to Jeff, but sporadically. I'd listen to each pass, always keeping in mind the greater whole of the show, and after some trial and error (though not much error at all), everyone came up with stuff that we felt good about.

My favorite band collaboration was on the song "What You Own." "Let's think about this as The Police meets Pearl Jam," I told them. I was only half sure about my approach, but that was the best analogy I could muster. As we started running through the tune, Kenny played a foundational Andy Summers, Police-like muted string part in the verses. And after I had sung the verses and indicated where to play the responses, Dan came up with an absolutely perfect melodic fragment on top of Kenny's muted string ostinato. I mean *perfect*, as if he had already heard Anthony and Adam sing the song. The pre-chorus grew out of the verse, and the chorus grew out of the pre-chorus, with Kenny producing a full-lead, arpeggiated, over-driven wall of sound that dared you to break through it. As if that weren't enough, on the bridge, Steph played a cross between a standard rock bass part and Henry Mancini's theme song from the old TV show *Peter Gunn*. It was subversive and fun, whimsical and serious. The coming together of that tune was something I'd never forget. It was the *Rent* band, in its earliest days, firing on all its creative cylinders.

Within the restrictive boundaries of musical theater, we were doing some high-level music making. And everyone in the band felt what was happening. These were musicians in their prime, with great taste and aesthetics born out of years of critical listening to music of all kinds, from classical to West African, Delta blues to ska, folk, funk, rock, R & B, and everything in between. They were so musically *sound!* The way we went about our business was traditional in the sense that there were a lot of notes on the page we were required to play, just as if we were doing *South Pacific*. But I'd told them early on about the grunge band concept, which meant we could jump comfortably into the rhythm section headspace of looking at some of the notes as suggestions, not final answers, the same approach I had taken with the band a year earlier. And so began everyone's creation of their own books. For the guitarists and bassist, this meant saying goodbye to a lot of the notes on the page and hello to chord changes and a more open musical canvas. They would color in their own style and taste as we went, and if we agreed it worked, we kept it. On we went, all of us doing what we had done our entire musical lives at endless numbers of gigs. The fact that we had less time and a harder deadline in the theater didn't matter to me. It wasn't finished until it was finished, I told them. And that's how the score of *Rent* came together, in the best combination of traditional and organic ways.

A seemingly random exchange that proved important to the development of the band came after the second day of rehearsal when Dan said to me, "You know, I think a lot of these tunes would sound really great on organ." He told me he had a Korg CX-3—a single-manual organ with drawbars, similar to the more well-known Hammond organ—and asked if he could try it on some of the songs.

"Sure," I said nonchalantly, not realizing that what was about to happen would be game-changing in terms of the soulfulness of our newly formed quintet. I didn't know it at the time, but Dan was a ridiculously talented organ player, influenced by Keith Emerson and Billy Preston, and what his organ playing brought to the sound of the band over those next few days was amazing. He improved on the already-written organ part for "Tango: Maureen" and created new ones for "Will I?" "Seasons of Love" A and B, "Take Me or Leave Me," and the "I'll Cover You" reprise. In addition to filling out Dan's book (frankly, he didn't initially have enough to play), the organ added colors that expanded the band's sound palette even further, and any rock, R & B, or gospel singer was more than happy to sing with some super-soulful organ behind them. We had an astonishing handful of rehearsals over those five days after the blizzard of '96, and we were ready to meet up with the cast for tech rehearsals the following week. That would be where all the separate elements of the show would come together as one. Hopefully.

Tech started on Tuesday, January 16, 1996. It began with cast only. The band would join us five days later. Tech rehearsal is where all the elements that fill in the production come together for the first time. Each director has their own idea of how they want their tech period to run. A lot of it depends on the show, but usually it begins with the physical set, which in our case was Paul Clay's responsibility. While we were finishing up our final week in the upstairs rehearsal room, Paul installed the set. Angela moved her costume operation from its offsite location to the theater, where her crew would strategically set up in places around the stage for costume changes, either routine or especially quick ones. She worked in concert with the hair and makeup departments, and they all worked in harmony to maximize their efficiency in a theater with limited offstage space and resources. Since everyone had a slightly bigger budget to work with than they'd had in 1994, every department had some room to expand and realize their visions a little further down their own creative road. The sound department moved in before the band, getting everything set up so folding the band into place would be easier. Since this time the band was a bit larger, Paul had designed the onstage band platform to accommodate all of us. Once the gear and amps were moved in, we were able to make some serious noise. Between the fifteen newly acquired wireless mics for the cast and the band gear, with amplification, in a theater with just under two hundred seats, the sound department was in for a huge challenge.

The sound department's issues were multiplied by some immovable audio realities. First, brick walls are a sound mixer's worst enemy, and the Workshop's theater had exposed brick on all four sides, including the back wall of the stage. Great for plays, bad for rock musicals. The sound ricocheted off those brick walls like a kangaroo on cocaine. Completely out of control. Then there was the shape of the theater. If you've ever been in a recording studio, one of the first things you'll notice is the shape of the recording rooms. Rectangular is pretty ideal, and an oddly shaped room opens up a lot of acoustical possibilities for the engineers. Anything but square. A square room creates an unequal distribution of sound and dead spots—a sound designer and engineer's nightmare. Sadly for us, the Workshop was square and brick. Two for two.

Musicals routinely run high on the decibel scale. A conversation at the dinner table for six people would be about fifty-five decibels. Our rock musical would easily surpass a hundred decibels in that relatively small house. A hundred and twenty decibels is like listening to a bulldozer or motorcycle up close. Arena rock concerts and auto racing are usually in the one hundred and forty to one hundred and fifty range. If you were a person who covered your ears on the subway, you would have been wise to stay away from our show. But there we were, the *Rent* band, ready to rock, and the fifteen mic'd up singers. We had an unenviable, maybe even unsolvable sonic problem in that theater, but with the excellent help of the sound team, we'd find our way through it. As long as most of the lyrics were understandable, we'd be fine, no matter the volume or intensity. It was a battle (more like hand-to-band combat) for the sound department from beginning to end, every day and night. No amplifiers were remote, and nothing was soundproofed by foam or plexiglass. Every instrument and speaker was fully open and moving a lot of air, literally.

When the band and cast performed together for the first time, all the magic the cast was making in the upstairs room and all the incredible things the band had done in rehearsals came together in a breathtaking way. No matter how much I could describe or sing the vocals to the band, there was nothing like them hearing and responding to the cast. The vocals were the glue to everything. The lyrics and melodies helped everyone in the band make connections that were otherwise unexplainable by me. Hearing Anthony and Adam sing "What You Own" helped Dan confirm his guitar part for the call and response in the verses. After the first line, "Don't breathe too deep," there were four beats in the clear, which was where Dan laid in his part. *Magic.* The excitement and the possibilities were infinite, just as they should have been. I had been through it in 1994, but not like *this*.

Tech was slow and tedious, particularly for some of the cast members who were new to the process. They were fidgety with all the stopping, starting, repeating, and standing still, but they soon learned they had to stay in their positions (for lighting) and to sing full-out when necessary (for sound). The show, especially act one, was deceptively difficult. This was still a nonprofit theater, so the cast had to move most of the tables and chairs with our skeleton crew, then get their costumes accessorized or changed, and be in their places for the start of the following scene. Making the difficult look effortless was essential to Michael's design and required an extraordinary level of detail. The many configurations of chairs and tables had to hit their exact marks so their multifunctionality would feel natural from scene to scene. There was magic to be made with costumes and lights alone. My personal favorite was the way Michael transitioned from the parents' "Voice Mail" quartet near the end of the second act into the seven-member homeless community. Under four bars of music and a blackout, one costume was peeled off another, the lights came up, and just like that there we were in a different location with different characters.

In the second week of tech, we put together larger chunks of the show. While the first act was incredibly challenging, act two was more straightforward. It always had been, even back when my friend Lonny saw the show. The hardest part of that second act was the song "Contact," which featured some complicated choreography and challenges for the sound department as they tried to squeeze as much clarity out of the lyrics as they could, spoken under a large bedsheet by everyone, in close contact. After the song ended, "Contact" segued into Angel's memorial service amid the eulogies spoken at the church, underscored by the intro to "Seasons of Love" as Angel exited offstage, figuratively and literally walking into the light. It was truly thoughtful and delicate staging that used the music as the connective tissue to facilitate that transition. That confluence of events, with music as its junction point, was a hallmark of Michael's direction. Jonathan, Michael, and Jim regarded the band as the sixteenth character in the cast. In my experience up until then, it was rare that the musicians played as vital (and visible) a role as we did. Jonathan's idea that Kenny's lead guitar was an extension of Roger's voice was genius (every one of Roger's songs is paired with either acoustic or electric guitar), and Michael reinforced that idea by placing the lead guitar closer to center stage than any other band member. I appreciated the three of them for the way we were folded into the show as equal partners.

During the time we spent in act two, Michael rehearsed "Take Me or Leave Me" quite a bit. I'm embarrassed to say that while we were rehearsing and running that song, I noticed that there was a hole where Fredi and Idina were holding a note at the end of the song, with only piano, organ, bass, and drums. There wasn't any other event offsetting that kind of staid moment during the four bars of the outro of the song. I asked Kenny, "Could you put in a guitar fill over those four bars where Fredi and Idina are holding that note?" Kenny, of course, was game for anything. Now the embarrassing part: over the next handful of passes, Kenny would try a fill, and apparently while I was looking down at the keyboard, I was unconsciously shaking my head a little, as if I was thinking, *No, that's not the one.* That continued for a few passes. Kenny would try a new fill, and my headshaking would silently disapprove. Then, on about the sixth try, Kenny landed on his iconic, funky, slightly offbeat, slightly traditional, all-original fill. Unbeknownst to me, on this try, I *nodded* my head in full agreement with his musical choice. Thankfully Kenny wasn't the least bit put off by my headshaking, head-nodding evaluations. I knew what I wanted when I heard it, but the unfortunate way I approached it was from the *How Not to Be a Bandleader* handbook. "Chapter One: Don't Communicate Directly with Anyone." It wasn't my best work by a mile, and yet somehow, in spite of me, it led to Kenny's perfect fill.

Tech rolled on toward the end of week two and was mostly uneventful for the band. The cast and the rest of the creative team, on the other hand, were constantly adjusting light cues, choreography, and the quicker costume changes—repeating and cementing their individual tracking. A dozen things happened simultaneously every time we ran even the smallest parts of the show. Our success was completely dependent upon the actors and crew working harmoniously, which over the previous two weeks had started to develop a rhythm of its own. Everything that happened on- and offstage could be seen by the entire audience, and so much of the show's forward motion depended on the transitions from one song to the next. Due to Michael's theatrical inventiveness, not one transition was like another. He employed the element of surprise, as well as a little craftiness, humor, and a lot of moving tables to delineate multiple locations. Side by side with those transitions were their close partners, the musical intros. Every song in the show had an intro (except the parents' voicemails and Maureen's performance piece, "Over the Moon"), which Michael used to his fullest advantage. I thought his use of the intros, vamps, or even a piece of underscoring helped give the evening its overall musical flow, despite the different tempos of the show's forty-six songs.

At last, there we were, good flow and all, at the end of two weeks of a difficult and rewarding tech period, with a show that felt as close to complete as we were going to get until previews. Once our audiences started coming, our work would continue. The week's schedule, right in front of us, would consist of rehearsals by day, a run-through on Tuesday night, an invited dress rehearsal on Wednesday night, and our first preview on Thursday night.

The cast, Michael, Jonathan, Martha, and me in front of the New York Theatre Workshop, 1995.

SUNDAY–MIDWEEK
January 21–24, 1996

AFTER SUNDAY'S AFTERNOON SESSION, we all went out for our dinner break. Many of us went to the Cooper Square Restaurant, which was a popular diner on Second Avenue, just north of the Workshop. A majority of the cast and a few of the creatives were there. Jonathan was there too. We had our meal and went back for the final hours of our long and grueling week. Even though it had been a significant amount of work, we were all in good spirits and that Sunday's dinner break would be our last meal together for the week. The following day we were off.

Before dinner we had gotten through the eulogies and the "I'll Cover You" reprise, a satisfying place to break. When we got back, we went through the transition out of the reprise to "Halloween," then to "Goodbye Love." It was all super detail-oriented and physically and mentally exhausting. Everyone had to be on their game. Sometimes as an antidote to the intensity of the work we were doing, in the right moment, I'd quietly noodle at the piano a little, whether it was to play the theme song from *The Simpsons* or *Mister Rogers' Neighborhood*, or a piece of a random song. While it was the caretaker in me trying to lighten the mood briefly, it was irritating to those who needed absolute quiet so they could concentrate on their work, so I'd stop before it got outright annoying. We came out of Daphne's exit at the end of "Goodbye Love" and made the deceptively tricky transition into a short scene and then into "What You Own," syncing the staging, lighting, and music to get Anthony smoothly into his first verse.

After multiple attempts we finally made it into the body of the song. Anthony and Adam didn't sing it full out because they knew they were going to have to sing it multiple times, but it was important for the sound guys to hear the band play it, so they could get a feel for the song as we had orchestrated it. We did it several times, as expected. It was getting toward 9:30 p.m. by then, so I knew there was no way we were going to make it to the end of the show. We still had a ways to go, but everything was cruising along nicely. Until it wasn't.

When we were more than halfway through "What You Own," Michael got on his director's mic and said, "Let's take a break everyone." It wasn't really time for a break, but I thought, great, maybe we could leave early after a long week. There was a noticeable quiet in the air. I came off the stage to head outside for a cigarette, and as I got to the back of the theater, there was Jonathan, behind the back row of the seats, lying face up on the floor, with a couple of paramedics standing over him. Apparently he had passed out, and Sue White had immediately called 911. Now conscious, he said, "Can you believe those guys are singing 'when you're dying in America,' and here I am?" There he was, the Jonathan I had come to know, summoning his flair for the ironic. It was one of his gifts. As it turned out, he was fine-ish, at least well enough to get through the evening. The paramedics hadn't found anything wrong with him and left, so we half-heartedly continued working. The first thing on everyone's mind, including Jonathan's, was that it must have been food poisoning—and no offense to diners, but a New York City diner is hardly among the most sterile places in America. (I knew this well because my first apartment was above one of them and I'd had the roaches and mice to prove it.) It was also possible that the food hadn't been cooked enough. While the creatives in the house proceeded with their difficult work, all the talk onstage was "What did you have?" "Jonathan had a turkey burger." "Did you have a turkey burger?" And on it went. No one was sick, thankfully, and soon our rehearsal came to an end. Everyone went home to rest up and have their day off, knowing what was ahead of us.

On Monday Jonathan went to an ER at a hospital in the West Village because he still didn't feel right. He was examined and had an X-ray taken and then was sent home by a doctor who told him to relax (good luck with that), drink fluids, take aspirin, and get some rest. Standard doctor's orders. It was late January in New York and we were deep into flu season, so that's what the doctor told Jonathan he probably had, which sounded completely plausible. Except no one had examined the X-ray.

Jonathan did as he was advised, but when I called him the next day and asked how he was doing, he told me, "I still feel terrible. I have to go back to the doctor."

This was early 1996, so people like Jonathan, the band, me, and probably most of the actors didn't have health care, much less a primary care physician. His only option, like for many of us, was to go to another ER at another hospital. There he got the same prescription: rest, fluids, aspirin. This was Tuesday, so I had to go to the Workshop to finish tech. Our hope was to stay on schedule with one last tech rehearsal in the afternoon session and our first run-through that night.

The next time I saw Jonathan was Wednesday night. I was onstage, getting my materials together, putting the score to act one on the music stand, and setting a blank notepad and pencil I kept to my left. When I looked to my right, there he was. He was dressed in the same green corduroy jacket he always wore, but he was pale as a mime. We've all been there, but I took notice because it had only been a few days since I'd seen him last, yet he looked like he was coming out of a serious ten-day bout with the flu, or worse. We chatted and I brought him up to speed on the work we'd done while he was away. Nothing earth-shattering, just a continuation of the work we had done Sunday night and the notes we had covered Tuesday and earlier Wednesday in preparation for that night's dress rehearsal. Pale as a mime, yes, but in good spirits considering he still felt crummy.

We did our first run for a small group of friends and colleagues to see. Some stuff went beautifully, some not so much, but most of it was solid. The cast was focused and the band was, as I expected, tight and professional. After we finished, Jonathan went up to Dan Weiss and told him, "I can't thank you enough. This is all I ever could have hoped for." Such kind words to someone he had never spoken to before. That was Jonathan. Even that previous Monday, sick as he was, he had called Martha to ask how she was feeling because she had also had the turkey burger. Amid a kind of stress and anxiety I couldn't have imagined, with his nagging bad health and the public showing of his big musical crossing paths, he still had the presence of mind, the consideration, the *decency* to call Martha and check in with her.

After the dress rehearsal the creative staff gathered in the audience, as was customary, for notes. This happened all the time, on every show through tech, run-throughs, and previews. There were a lot of things that revealed themselves as we did the show in real time, and those post-performance notes sessions were an incredibly valuable tool for us to figure out what needed attention. I loved those notes sessions. The director was in charge, but every department had our own to-do lists and got to give their input. If I had to work some stuff out with the actors, those notes sessions were where we would schedule time to address them the following day. Notes sessions were always weighty, stressful, helpful, and exhilarating.

While Michael gave out his notes, Jonathan was finishing

up an interview with the classical music critic from the *New York Times*, Anthony Tommasini. Anthony had heard about *Rent* from a colleague at the *Times* and he thought an interview with Jonathan about the show, coinciding with the hundredth anniversary of *La bohème*, would make a good piece. Apparently he liked the show very much. As he interviewed Jonathan in the small lobby of the Workshop, the band trundled through, stashing their six guitars, two basses, multiple pedals, and bags of drumsticks, cables, and keyboard accessories in a storage area above the theater's box office. There were a lot of "Excuse me, sorry, excuse me please, pardon me" apologies. I could easily picture the dichotomy of Jonathan doing his once-in-a-lifetime interview and the band doing their once-every-night storage routine.

After the interview Jonathan joined us for the final notes with a few of his own to share, mostly sound-related. He had a few notes for me but said we could go over them tomorrow. Then Michael set the plan for the following day of rehearsal before our first preview the next night. Getting through any tech period and a first run-through was an accomplishment unto itself, so we all felt good. I was looking forward to our first preview for our first paying audience. For those of us in the band or orchestra, performing was always a little bit easier, less nerve-wracking. I'd be playing and/or conducting the next night, just as I'd been doing all along. Jonathan, Michael, the other creatives, and the producers could only watch, with no control over the outcome. I looked at my silver Motorola flip phone: it was 12:40 a.m. We said our good nights and walked out into the winter. As I got into a taxi headed uptown, I watched Jonathan walk toward his beat-up blue 1980s Datsun station wagon.

Jonathan drove back to his West Village apartment at 508 Greenwich Street. He probably walked into the apartment sometime after 1:00 a.m. We'd later learn that after he arrived he put on a pot of water for tea. His roommate came home somewhere between 3:00 and 3:30 a.m. and found Jonathan lying on the floor, dead, and the tea kettle dry-whistling on the stove.

"Would you light my candle?" Daphne and Adam at the New York Theatre Workshop, 1996.

NOW WHAT?

January 25—February 13, 1996

A FEW MONTHS LATER—I have a blurry recollection of the exact timeline—we started hearing from Jonathan's father, Al, and Jonathan's close friends that Jonathan might have had a congenital disorder called Marfan syndrome, a condition that compromises the connective tissue in the body, leading to abnormalities in the eyes, skeleton, heart, and blood vessels. The most potentially life-threatening aspect of this condition is its effect on the aorta—the largest artery that carries blood from the heart to the rest of the body. As a result of Marfan syndrome, the aorta stretches or enlarges—this is called an aneurysm—and if the condition goes unrecognized and untreated, an aortic dissection—a tear in the wall of the aorta—can occur, which can be fatal. While that may have been what caused Jonathan's death in the early hours of Thursday, January 25, no one knew any of that, including the coroner. When Sue told me what had happened, I was stunned. That phone call was gut-wrenching.

After I hung up, I left the apartment and drifted to the subway and took my usual route to the Workshop, I guess. There were few people at the theater when I arrived. Michael and Jim were still at a breakfast meeting nearby, at the Time Café on

Lafayette and East Fourth, their locale for many pre-rehearsal morning meetings. They were surely figuring out what was in front of them and how we would proceed that day. I say "that day" because now every day would be "that day" until we collectively staggered back to our feet. Or "that day" would be a few hours at a time. Who could know? I slumped down in one of the aisle seats near the back of the theater, numb and motionless, barely moving for the entire morning. Soon people from the Workshop drifted in. Sue, Martha, Kate, and Linda, then Michael and Jim. More numbness, sadness, and immobility. Surreal doesn't even begin to explain how the theater felt. I wasn't in any kind of working headspace. That all went out the door into the cold late-January morning. My head and heart were screaming in unison, *I can't fucking believe it. I can't fucking believe it. How the fuck did this happen? Fuck, fuck, FUUUCCK!* I slammed my fist into my score repeatedly. I sat there, unable to do or think about anything, utterly helpless and stuck in a present I didn't want to be in. Yet there I was.

Around 11:30 I pulled myself up and went around the corner to the cool little Middle Eastern takeout place where Jonathan and I had gotten many of our lunches during rehearsal. It was a typical hole-in-the-wall joint with the same guy—probably the owner—working there six days a week, but they served killer Middle Eastern food. Chicken or falafel with hummus, tahini, and tabouli jammed into a delicious pita pocket. I cried when I ordered. The dude behind the counter said nothing. Didn't matter. I took my food back to the theater, to my seat on the aisle. I had always eaten either upstairs, in the kitchen adjacent to the rehearsal room, sometimes with Jonathan, or, while we were in tech, on the aisle steps in the theater. Like always, the food was delicious and comforting. Jonathan being gone didn't make the chicken less sweet or the tahini less savory. I needed a little solace in that moment more than anything.

MAKING RENT

As the morning turned to early afternoon, more people started drifting in. There were some folks that I knew and some unfamiliar faces. The cast, some outsiders, and, as I came to learn, Jonathan's close circle of New York friends. Jonathan had told me a lot about them, and I'd looked forward to meeting them—but not like this. They had been there for Jonathan during every step of his long journey. They had even paid for some of his electronic music-making gear. He'd described them as the best, tightest circle of friends one could have. The fog of shock, pain, and agony they felt was visible and thick. Like me, they were stunned. But underneath it all, as I would find out later, they knew their friend would want his show to go on. This was what he had lived for, they said. They knew his dreams, what he'd wanted, and who he'd aspired to be. They knew he would have wanted to have his musicals in the pantheon of the American musical theater canon, next to those of Sondheim and Rodgers and Hammerstein, the best of the best. The respect and empathy they showed to the cast moved me deeply. Jonathan's friends knew that the *Rent* cast was his dream come true, and even though he had passed away, we had to press ahead, no matter the outcome.

By 3:00 p.m. we knew it was time to begin to move from wherever we all were to somewhere else. There was work to be done. Jim had a responsibility to his crew, company, and staff to implement a plan for moving forward. The *Rent* train had left the station. It may have sounded cold in light of Jonathan's passing, but unless Jim heard otherwise from the Larson family, everything was as it was the previous night, with an urgency to keep moving forward. If a time came when the Larson family wanted to shut it all down, Jim would have done it. But without that, he and Michael had come up with a solution for how we, as a company, would proceed that Thursday evening.

At the time the first act was still about an hour and forty-five minutes long. The constant moving of the chairs and tables, the tricky musical staging involving all fifteen cast members, not to mention the choreography, added up to a lot of congestion. Between the logistics of the show and the day's emotional upheaval, a full performance would have been too much to take on. Since we still had some technical and safety issues to be concerned with, Michael wisely decided to memorialize and celebrate Jonathan with a simple presentation of his amazing score, the actors sitting in chairs at tables. I thought Michael and Jim's plan was solid. Just present the cast, the band, and Jonathan's songs. Everyone would understand. This situation was tragic and different and required a thoughtful and safe approach to the unthinkable, impossible circumstances of that evening's presentation.

So there we all sat that afternoon in a circle on the stage where we would perform Jonathan's work. Eventually, people started sharing a few of their own experiences, remembrances, and exchanges they'd had with Jonathan over the previous two months. I volunteered to share, and then I lost it. I *bawled.* Loudly. Uncontrollably. Niagara Falls, full-blown, full-grown sorrow pouring out from me before I collapsed onto Taye, this young man I barely knew. I was hysterical, but what I truly felt was deep anguish, a sadness and despair that I had never known. Thankfully, Taye just held me in his arms. I don't remember for how long. It was for as long as I needed before I could sit up on my own.

Everything Jonathan and I had done together came rushing to my mind. All the music we had talked about, agreed and disagreed about, even argued about, and all we had come to understand about each other. We were around the same age, in similar circumstances. I think we both felt like we had our noses pressed against the window of the commercial theater, looking in. Yes, we both had a good history of professional writing and music making, but we also had the same gaping hole that *Rent* was filling. Along with Michael, Jim, the Workshop, our fellow creatives, and this incredible cast, we were executing our shared vision about the kind of musical theater we wanted to do, and it was all coming together in a big way. Just a month earlier, Jonathan had said to me, "I've found my collaborator!" At that time I didn't quite know what he meant. But Jonathan knew on a deep level that we were kindred musical spirits, as respectful of pop and rock as we were of contemporary musical theater. That was our bond. I sobbed for the loss of my newest friend, and for my former, not future, collaborator.

I remember feeling that even though I was the musical director and was supposed to be a pillar for the company, nothing mattered but the deep pain of Jonathan's passing. I hoped my vulnerability and willingness to reveal my emotional truth would somehow make me a stronger leader, a more trustworthy partner, as we dove into waters none of us had been in before. And after the wailing and howling, after the tidal wave of immense, intense sadness passed, I did start, slowly, to feel the first morsels of a renewed strength coming on—a focus, determination, and, frankly, an unfamiliar self-assuredness that I was ready to meet the moment, whatever happened. I no longer had Jonathan in the flesh, but I still had my collaborators riding with me: Michael and our creative team, Jim and everyone at NYTW, the cast, and, of course, the band.

The feeling in the theater that evening was sheer pain, utter sadness, helplessness, and mourning. All of it hung thick in the air. The audience was almost full. Jonathan's New York friends were there, as well as his Los Angeles friends, some of whom had flown in. The Workshop's staff and friends were there as well. The seats with the tape around them were reserved for Jonathan's parents, Allan and Nanette Larson—Al and Nan—who had received the worst news a parent could ever hear. Earlier that day they had gotten the first flight they could from their home in Albuquerque. Julie, who had been visiting them, flew with them, and Julie's husband, Chuck, flew in from Los Angeles. There were also plenty of aunts, uncles, and cousins in New York, New Jersey, and Connecticut who made it to the Workshop for what had become a somber occasion.

We were soon onstage. The band entered casually and got situated, but instead of the cast entering with purpose and energy, arriving at their assigned places onstage, that night they all entered slowly, eerily quiet, and found their places in their newly assigned chairs. The atmosphere was heavy. I wasn't nervous, just morose and prepared for anything. Maybe some stopping and starting, maybe not. But those were things that I would have expected from a fully realized performance of the show, not the concert memorial we were about to present.

And so we began. Mark's narration, the "Tune Ups," then into "Rent." It rocked, but like the cast, I felt it just sat there. Yes, after we finished "Rent" there was applause, but it sounded almost perfunctory. The opening fifteen minutes of the show were where I felt Jonathan's absence the most. Maybe a lot of us were feeling that, because as the next couple of songs came and went, everything felt blank and lifeless. Then when Adam started singing "One Song Glory," something happened. It was small, but it *happened*. As he sang and as the cast and audience absorbed the lyrics, a nerve was hit in the theater.

> One song glory,
> one song before I go.
> Glory.
> One song to leave behind.

I could feel it and I could hear that Adam was lighting the song up. He sang with a passion and a connection to the character and the lyric that I hadn't heard before. Then he got to the end and the lyric "Time flies, and then no need to endure anymore. Time dies," and the tone for what was to come, even under controlled circumstances, was set. It was tragically apparent to everyone who knew what had transpired in the previous twenty-four hours that art was imitating life. For the cast, from that point forward, the characters they were playing were intersecting with their lived experience. Whatever they couldn't, or wouldn't, express that afternoon was channeled through their remarkable and unshakable performance that night. It was all so chilling and reassuring, so life-altering and life-affirming. This was the first time I truly understood that both sadness and joy could exist at the same time. Sorrow and celebration. Obstacles and triumph. And as it turned out, the cast was just getting started.

My ears couldn't believe what I was hearing, but the cast was still seated. The fact that they could summon that kind of vocal energy and still be in their chairs sounded, appropriately, otherworldly. We eventually arrived at "La Vie Boheme," a song that begins in a slightly tame way musically, but has a slow, powerful build as the couples start their verses after Mark's solo—first Mimi and Angel, then Maureen and Collins, and so on. Everyone, knowing their bodies couldn't remain stagnant any longer, started getting up from their chairs and took the song to the tabletops, where they danced, sang, and celebrated all that Jonathan loved about the bohemian life. It was like they had been in a glass-enclosed space for the first act, then collectively blew it to smithereens, and another level of exuberance and escape, purpose and *fun* entered the theater. It was magical. I habitually kept half an eye on the cast, but I couldn't see everything that was happening. It wasn't necessary to see it—the energy erupted so quickly and so passionately that it consumed everyone in its presence. A howling release that was remarkably both personal and connective. I was in such awe that they felt the collective inspiration and freedom to be so brave, trusting, and unabashedly celebratory. I believe they were galvanized by Jonathan's music and each other, and it was beautiful.

Back in the dressing rooms, Michael asked the cast if they wanted to perform the second act as rehearsed rather than returning to their seats onstage. Act two was much safer to execute—not as frenetically paced as the first act—and we had run it successfully multiple times prior to that night. Of course, the cast said yes. After "La Vie Boheme," how could they come out and sit down again? The band was ready, and I played Jonathan's beautiful opening chords to "Seasons of Love." The cast came out through their entrances, formed their line, and sang, pouring their hearts into it. For a moment I flashed back to the first time they all sang the song together at rehearsal, after Gwen was added in. I was busy music directing, listening, making sure it all hung together, doing my job. Now I heard its sheer beauty and message as if for the first time.

After the final song ended, and since Michael hadn't staged the curtain call yet (it was supposed to have happened during that afternoon's rehearsal), the cast bowed informally and acknowledged the band, to the sound of applause, I guess. I don't remember hearing it. But unlike on the evenings that would follow—when, after the bows, the cast would exit and the band would play the exit music—everyone just stood there. The clapping stopped and dead silence consumed the theater. After what felt like, I don't know, fifteen seconds or fifteen minutes, someone in the audience called out, "Thank you, Jonathan Larson!" For a moment, the sadness was lifted just enough so people could exhale and get up from their seats. I noticed a lot of Jonathan's friends and family members congregating around the people I suspected were his parents, and Julie, Chuck, and his aunts, uncles, and cousins, who were still seated. I saw introductions being made, lots of hugging. Some joy, but mostly pain. While I had most felt Jonathan's absence in the first fifteen minutes of the first act, I suspect most of the audience felt it hardest after the show ended.

We did meet for notes after everyone had straggled out of the theater; it was obvious we had a lot to do. There was, of course, the elephant in the room: should we, could we, proceed without the family's blessing? That question had, unbeknownst to all of us, already been answered by Jonathan's father, Al. At intermission, he'd said to one of the producers, Jeffrey Seller, "You must do this play. You need to do this play. Your job is to do this play." Jim had already scheduled a meeting for nine o'clock the next morning with Michael, Lynn, and me. Michael believed Jonathan would have wanted us to continue making his work as good as we could and make him proud. The show, act one in particular, was still too long and needed some major cuts as well as a little snipping and trimming in other places. Jim's role as artistic director was to take care of the Workshop's staff, crew, and management team, as well as the cast, because until he heard otherwise, he was still on a schedule to begin previews, now one night later than originally planned. The next morning's meeting would mark the beginning of the mission going forward.

On Friday at 9:00 a.m. the four of us met in Jim's office. There was plenty to do before the cast came in later that day. We still didn't have an opening that we were happy with, Michael and Jim especially. We knew we had to have a great first fifteen minutes of the show and we didn't have it yet. The problem, still unsolved, was our highest priority.

Jonathan, for a long while during the 1994 version and into the early stages of the 1995–96 production, had held on to his firm belief that the show could be told in flashback, starting with the song "Halloween." I don't remember how many versions of "Halloween" he wrote in service of that notion. At least a half dozen, and each one began with dialogue over the "Halloween" music before Mark would eventually sing, "How did we get here? How the hell? Christmas! Christmas Eve last year." I knew Jonathan believed strongly in his idea, but he eventually figured out that for whatever reason, it just wasn't going to work, and not for lack of effort on his part. One morning, after finishing his newest version, he had called me and exclaimed, "I've got it! See you soon!"

When I'd met him at the theater I'd asked if I could look at it, and he'd responded, "I threw it out on my way over." I think that was the morning he officially gave up on the whole flashback concept. For the rest of rehearsal and tech we had just opened the show with "Tune Up A." However, this is one of the many things I loved about Jonathan. His conviction to never give up on an idea he was sure of, his willfulness, his determination, and, yes, his stubbornness. "Yeah, dude," you wanted to say to him. "But you can't do it. Not this time. Let it go." He did, but he'd fully intended to revisit the opening, with help from Lynn and Michael if necessary. And now, the second morning after Jonathan's passing, here we were. Jonathan had written the "Tune Ups," but as clever as they were, they didn't rise to the lofty standard of an opening number to a musical.

The problem, as Michael correctly saw it, was that the show was about a community of people in the East Village, and with the "Tune Ups" we met only a small handful of characters. Great songs, but still a much smaller subsection of the whole. On that Friday morning in Jim's office, the spitballing began. Jim said to me, "Tim, can you maybe try making the 'Tune Ups' faster? It all just feels slow." I could've done that, but I knew that wasn't the best solution. A faster tempo would have required a bit more guitar virtuosity from Adam, since the guitar in that song was played by him live, and it would have sounded a little goofy. There was a lot of important exposition that couldn't be missed in those songs, and they also served as a kind of musical prologue before Mark, Roger, Collins, Benny, and then the rest of the community (including the band) slammed their collective fist right into the audience's sternum with "Rent." If the "Tune Ups" were too fast, the musical onslaught of "Rent" would be less explosive. I said none of this because I already had an idea in my mind.

The nice folks in the office set up a workspace for me on the Workshop's second floor, and I got down to it. The first thing I'd ever noticed about the "Tune Ups" was that they were all in 4/4 time. Four beats to the measure, quarter note gets one beat. My first and best answer to making the song seem like it was going faster was to trim a beat or two, or three, wherever I could. Early in "Tune Up A," Mark sings, "So we hear. / He's just coming back . . . " In that lyric, "hear" was the only word of a 4/4 measure (also called a bar), so the lyric was followed by three empty beats over the rest of the bar. That early in the song, those three empty beats made it feel slow, exactly as Jim had expressed. The audience would already be ahead of the dialogue in a small way before the next line, so I cut those beats and made it a 2/4 bar instead. Less space. Next lyric: "Are you talking to me? / Not at all." Again, after the lyric "Are you talking to me?" there were two extra beats of nothing. The audience is ahead of the conversation again, and so on. Those little pauses might not seem like much when considered individually, but they interrupted the natural flow of the sung dialogue and accumulated awkwardly over the course of the song. I didn't expect the audience to understand what was happening either musically or intellectually. It wasn't their job. It was just about how they felt. They could feel when they were a little ahead of the conversation, when they were waiting for us to catch up. That is *the* important axiom for those of us who help create musical theater: don't let the audience get ahead of you. I had known that for a long time, but this was the first show where I put it to good use. A nip here, a tuck there. That was the beginning of a lot of nipping and tucking.

The first place I ever heard that sort of rhythmic twist was from the band Tower of Power, one of the great soul, funk, and jazz bands, on their 1972 track "Down to the Nightclub." The song was soulful and funky, everything I loved—but the moment before every chorus had always sounded a little odd to me. Not wrong, just striking. After listening a bunch of times, I realized that in this 4/4 song, at the end of every verse two beats were cut, creating a 2/4 bar. It was almost as if the record had skipped, but it felt tight, tasteful, and naturally funky. That's the first time I noticed beats deliberately cut out of a song. In the opposite way, the most famous (in my opinion) *additional* beat appears in The Beatles's "Don't Let Me Down," in which every verse begins with John Lennon singing a 5/4 bar. While it's metrically odd, it feels completely natural. The origins of pop music's jagged rhythms date back to the Delta blues musicians of the early twentieth century, so any variations in rhythms or the number of beats in a bar of music are on solid footing where tradition is concerned. Those are just two examples I had learned early in my musical life, and here I was about twenty years later applying one of them to *Rent*. What I was doing in those moments reaffirmed that all the music I had consumed—via record, cassette, CD, or live performance, for pleasure or as a private study—had been presented to me by teachers, those legions of musicians who passed on their wisdom through their artistry.

 I brought my homework back into the rehearsal room, where I played and sang it for Jim and Michael. They both really liked it, and so, just like that, it was in the show. While I was at it, I had done the same thing with the three other "Tune Ups." One box checked off, but it still wasn't the opening we wanted. That would come later. What I didn't know while working that morning was that Jim was considering the options laid out before him. What would be the most ethical approach to finishing the show, since we had lost our composer and lyricist? Should we interview and hire a replacement songwriter? After much consternation, and maybe encouraged a little by my updated "Tune Up," Jim realized that it would take too long to bring a new person up to speed and that nobody could know this material as thoroughly as we all did.

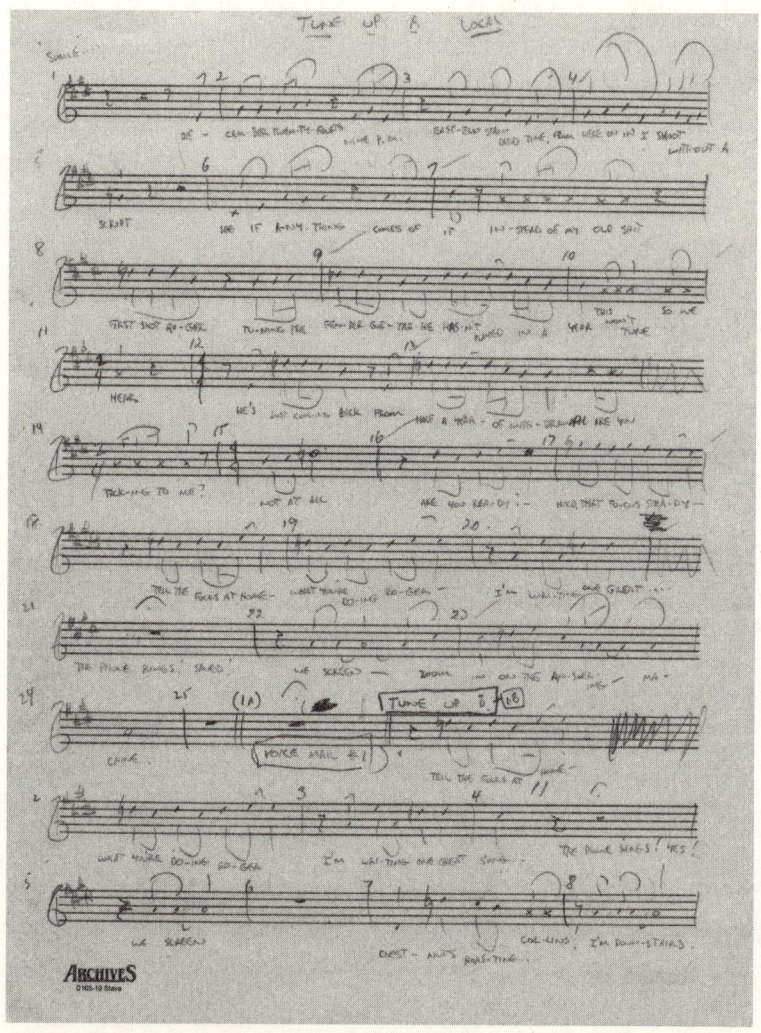

My rewrite of "Tune Up A." Friday, January 26, 1996.

Lynn knew it dramaturgically, since she had been working with Jonathan for about a year by then. Michael knew it dramaturgically as well, having worked with Jonathan for almost two years, and he had a clear vision for what the piece should look and feel like. He knew and understood Jonathan's aesthetic better than anyone. And for my part, I was more than confident that I had absorbed and understood Jonathan's musical vocabulary; however nimble we had to be with the score, I'd be up to it. For Jim it was a morally sound decision to not bring on anyone else, but he knew he had to give it serious consideration before we set off on this new phase together, because it was the right thing to do. That was Jim through and through: thinking everything through for everyone's sake—the family, NYTW, its board of directors, and everyone else he would have to answer to.

We had a little more than two weeks to make changes with the cast, band, and the other departments, particularly lights, costumes, and sound, as well as the rest of the crew. With so many changes flying into the show, the cast needed as many repetitions as possible. It would have been a boatload of new material to sing and act in the best of times, but now it had become a much heavier emotional lift as well. This is where that amazing, resilient, talented cast really showed up. While they were all grieving in their own ways, separately and together, we were all as hyper-focused on the task at hand over those next two weeks as we'd ever been.

Days bled into each other, and all we could do was press onward. More trimming, no matter how infinitesimal. Nothing was too small or out of bounds. The entire show had to be tightened up wherever possible, except where Michael deemed it impossible. For instance, I would have loved to edit the intro to the first "Christmas Bells" motif, but that wasn't going to happen. Between the end of "Rent" and his brief solo, Byron, playing a homeless man, had to run up the stairs to the top of the platform, add some costume pieces on the way, and get to his position at the front corner of the railing. That staging took four full bars of solo piano, even after the usually lengthy applause after "Rent" had ended, before he could be in place to sing "Christmas bells are ringing." To cover the four-bar intro, Michael had the shrewd theatrical idea to have Angel drum on a plastic pickle tub on the junk sculpture across the stage. Not only did it accompany the piano intro and distract from Byron's journey, the drumming also subtly introduced the audience to a new character before the scene that followed. Artful and practical stagecraft by Michael, staying ahead of the audience in his own way. Before Collins and Angel sang "You Okay Honey?" we tightened up the pickle tub solo and got into the song quicker. Not much, but every little bit helped. I made a tiny cut in "Voice Mail #2" of two beats, then cut two bars at the end of every chorus of "You'll See." Over the course of more than two weeks of previews, I'd go through the score, trim where I could, run the cuts past Michael, and together we'd see if the pacing was better. The show, especially act one, still felt long. The running time itself wasn't the problem—the act sometimes just lost its forward motion—but Michael would address those larger structural issues in time.

As much progress as we were making, there was still the elephant in the musical: the opening. The Tuesday morning after our first weekend of performances, we were meeting in Jim's office and he was paging through the beginning of Jonathan's libretto, which contained Jonathan's author's notes. Some were neatly typewritten, but mostly they were a lot of scribbles in the margins, which was consistent with Jonathan's lyric-writing process. I could picture him reading what he had typed, then adding in handwritten specificity. His notes contained ideas about the setting (Mark and Roger's loft, not too dissimilar from his own apartment), the neighborhood, character bios, and his overall vision of the show. Jim, looking all this over, wondered aloud if Jonathan's notes could be fashioned into an opening, a kind of prologue. After rehearsal Michael took that material home and crafted it into what became Mark's monologue at the beginning of the musical:

> We begin on Christmas Eve, with me, Mark, and my roommate, Roger. We live in an industrial loft on the corner of Eleventh Street and Avenue B, on the top floor of what was once a music-publishing factory. Old rock 'n' roll posters hang on the wall. They have Roger's picture advertising gigs at CBGB's and the Pyramid Club. We have an illegal wood-burning stove; its exhaust pipe crawls up to a skylight. All of our electric appliances are plugged into one thick extension cord which snakes its way out a window. Outside, a small tent city has sprung up in the lot next door to our building. Inside, we're freezing because we have no heat. Smile!

Mark, as the narrator, brings the audience into the show, with speech, then song. He's the only character who regularly does both. He plays the role of host, the audience's tour guide, and at various points throughout the show, he lets the audience know what's happened or what's about to happen. He's the "you are here" red dot on a map. As a great byproduct of this new "prologue," the other moments in the show when Mark narrates didn't feel like they came out of thin air because the opening monologue had set the precedent. And sure enough, Michael brought it into rehearsal and it fit like a glove, like it had been there from the beginning.

By the end of the first full week of previews, all was going well. But the first act was still uncomfortably long and that was when Michael began to implement the larger cuts to the songs that he had clearly been thinking about for a while. Had Jonathan still been with us he would have done the same thing.

A brief aside, if I may. All music—pop, rock, R & B, country, and so on—is built on structures that have existed since at least the Baroque era of classical music in the seventeenth century. At their most complicated, these structures can hold up massive pieces of music, like symphonies and operas. But the earliest and simplest musical structure is a song form we call ABA. "A" is one section of music. It is followed by a second "B" section, which is then followed by repeating the A section. The ABA form gives us symmetry and balance, which gives the music a comfortable, satisfying feeling to most of us. As music developed over centuries, song forms became more complex. Fast-forward to contemporary popular music and you'll still find the letters A and B, but they are joined by a litany of new letters and words to help further define the building blocks of this music.

Here's how this might break down: the intro is the beginning of the song. Usually it's only instrumental music, but in rare cases it has lyrics as well. The intro is followed by the verse, or the A section, which tells the story of the song. The number of verses is determined by the depth of the storytelling, but in most songs there are between two and four verses. After the A section comes the chorus, or the B section. This section is the catchiest musically and often contains the title of the song, usually repeated. Before the chorus there will sometimes be a pre-chorus, or the A1 section. This is fairly self-explanatory—a link after the verse and before the chorus—and is usually the shortest part of a song. Not all songs have them, but they do appear in some of the songs in *Rent* ("You'll See" and "Out Tonight," to name two). The triumvirate of the verse, pre-chorus, and chorus most often happens twice before proceeding to the new section, the bridge, or the C section. Most often the bridge will impart new information, history, or perspective, and its music is different from everything that preceded it but is still connected to the rest of the song harmonically. The song rides out with repeated choruses, which either fade out, as on most recordings, or are buttoned up by a coda, a short section that leads to the song's end. *Coda* is the Italian word for "tail."

This structure—intro, verse, chorus, verse, chorus, bridge, chorus (sometimes repeated and faded), coda—has stood the test of time, alongside its earliest counterpart, the ABA form from the Baroque era, mostly because of its symmetry and balance. It can be altered, expanded, or truncated in any imaginable way, but there is a reason Western music has relied on these forms for so many centuries. They're dependable and orderly, yet flexible, with a splash of chaos, a pretty good reflection of Western society itself.

All Michael had was the work that Jonathan had written. Nothing new was coming in. Jim's decision to not bring anyone else onboard had been made, so the answers to the puzzle of the show lay within the work that was already onstage. Michael knew the rules and regulations of modern musical theater, and he didn't mess with them. For him it was all about the show's ability to self-propel and never become static. If there were parts of songs that didn't move the plot forward or reveal character, those sections were fair game for cutting. As masterful as Jonathan's songwriting was, there were verses, pre-choruses, and even whole choruses of songs that were repetitive, so every song needed to be seen through the prism of lyrical content while trying to keep Jonathan's structures intact, or at least symmetrical.

The first big cut was obvious. "Out Tonight," in Mimi's loft, had an extra verse and pre-chorus, both of which were easy to lose. Since all the sections in that song were abnormally long, cutting a twenty-four bar verse and an eight-bar pre-chorus were, as the expression goes, low-hanging fruit. I felt my responsibility was to be the structure police. If I felt the structural integrity of any of Jonathan's songs was compromised, I'd bring it up to Michael for him to consider. In "Tango: Maureen," Michael proposed that we cut the entire second verse and second chorus. The musician in me was, let's say, bothered—but *outraged* is more on the money. I was so used to songs having at least two verses (think Billy Joel's "New York State of Mind"), or two of anything, before a song changed direction. That idea had been sewn into my musician's brain since I learned The Beatles's "Let It Be" as a twelve year old. I felt a song generally had to earn the right to get to the chorus or the bridge.

Still, we put Michael's large cut into "Tango: Maureen," and of course it was fine. Here's what Michael understood that the musician in me didn't: what followed the song's intro was entirely balanced. There was the verse, chorus, bridge, interlude, verse, chorus, then coda. So the interlude, which contained a tango-style dance break with dialogue, became the fulcrum of the entire song, keeping it in balance. Michael saw the superstructure in a way that I hadn't. It was, in its own way, symmetrical and harmonious. Even though it didn't fit the traditional pop musical structure, the song was successful on every other level. I couldn't believe I had an emotional response to upsetting a song's structure, but I also felt my inner caretaker tapping me on the shoulder, reminding me to protect Jonathan's work. Michael was too, but from a different point of view. I learned a little something there, and after I got used to the new version, I realized that it no longer sagged and we'd cut a minute and a half off the song. I had come to more fully understand Michael's approach by then, and I trusted him even more, if that was possible.

We made a similar cut in "Another Day." Roger sang his side of the argument, then Mimi sang her response, "The heart may freeze / or it can burn," into what I called the Mimi chorus, "There's only us, there's only this," ending with Jonathan's iconic lyric "No day but today." Michael smartly suggested that after Roger sang his second verse, we cut Mimi's second verse and get right to the Mimi chorus, where the real important lyrical meat on the bone lay. It also ended with "No day but today," which made total sense to me, it being Mimi's mantra. Then I just had to figure out the musical edit to get from the end of Roger's second verse into the second Mimi chorus. I changed Roger's melody a bit and inserted a Jonathan-esque chord to facilitate the transition, lopping off another thirty-five seconds or so and again trimming some fat off the song.

Next, Michael asked me to cut the last bar of "Life Support" and segue directly into "Out Tonight." Ruefully, I agreed. The last chord of the original "Life Support" was pure Jonathan, haunting and gorgeous, but, yeah, theatrically unnecessary. Michael's instinct was right on the nose, even if I'd need a minute to lament that beautiful chord's passing. I changed the group vocal a bit at the very end and Michael made a hard, cinematic cut to the following scene in Mimi's loft for "Out Tonight."

There was one place where we drew the line. We talked a bit about cutting "We're Okay," the song where Joanne is in a vacant lot talking on two phones at once. It's a great song, funny and charming, and we learn a little more about Joanne, but since we were feeling the pressure of cutting some of the first act, that was the one that showed up as the best candidate to cut. In the end it stayed because cutting it would have been a bridge too far. It wasn't what Jonathan would've wanted. We couldn't justify that all the work we were doing was in Jonathan's best interest, then turn around and cut a song he wouldn't ever want to lose. Michael was smart to keep it in. We needed a break, a new character, a new location, and a new musical feel after the section that included "On the Street," "Santa Fe," and "I'll Cover You," all songs with similar feels and tempos. We tried going directly from "I'll Cover You" into "Christmas Bells," but that didn't feel right. Also, "We're Okay" had the same musical theme and feel as the

MAKING RENT

Joanne section in the song "Rent." Structurally, that mattered. It was an easy thing to do, all things considered. We kept the song in—something I was happy about because it was as close to "Green Onions" as the show would ever get.

The last and most prodigious cuts were saved for "La Vie Bohème" through to the end of the first act. First, we cut a verse in the middle of the song when the entire cast comes in. This, we kept:

> Bisexuals, trisexuals, Homo sapiens,
> Carcinogens, hallucinogens, men, Pee-wee Herman.
> German wine, turpentine, Gertrude Stein, Antonioni, Bertolucci,
> Kurosawa, "Carmina Burana!"

This, we cut:

> CBGB's, De La Soul, tabouli, body fluids,
> KS lesions, spotty lungs, transfusions, silence equals death.
> Baudrillard, Derrida, Bertolt Brecht, de Kooning, Cannabis sativa,
> Camel Lights, Carmen Miranda, Nirvana!

Before segueing into the song "I Should Tell You," there is an interlude where Mimi and Roger find out they both have AIDS. Then they begin the song, which originally had a musical intro twice as long, followed by four verses, two pre-choruses, and two choruses, before landing on the "here goes" section. I use the word *section* because it wasn't just the six times they ultimately sang it in the show. It was a section. A repetitive, seemingly unending *section*. Again, great songwriting, but way too much romantic ballad so late in the act. I was itching for it to end while I was playing it. Michael suggested we make the following edits, which we did: a four-bar intro, which I set on acoustic guitar to musically announce this new episode, two verses instead of four, one pre-chorus, one chorus, and, finally, the paring down of the "here goes" section.

Jonathan had made a significant cut and rewrite from the end of "I Should Tell You" to the end of the act. In the 1994 version there had been a musical interlude called "La Vie–Coda" that underscored Roger and Mimi's kiss as the snow gently fell upon them. It was very theatrical and would have been great for the New York City Opera. I knew what Jonathan was shooting for—a heavenly orchestration without vocals that would accompany beautiful visuals as the scene unfolded elegantly. That was never going to happen with our little four-piece band at the New York Theatre Workshop. Jonathan cut the piece, then replaced it with new lyrics and end-of-the-act plot details that carried us effortlessly into "La Vie Boheme B." Joanne, who had been sent to pack up the sound equipment at the lot, returns to the Life Café to announce that a riot has broken out on Avenue B in response to Maureen's performance. The news is the catalyst for the rest of the song to kick into overdrive, first in pairs, then collectively—as I built the vocal arrangement into what I hoped would be a satisfying ending to the song. In the perfect bookend to act one, Mark, as narrator, takes us home, just as he brings us in at the top of the show, before a final celebratory exclamation from the entire community, "*Viva la vie bohème!*"

Jonathan's work in 1995, the new musical cuts, Michael's feel for pacing and staging, and Marlies's choreography, had turned "La Vie Boheme" from a twenty-five- minute marathon into a thirteen-minute romp. The icing on the cake was that, with a big nod to Kenny, we solved the riot issue. Obviously the entire cast was partying at the Life Café, so they weren't a part of it, but the audience needed visual evidence that a riot was happening outside. The theatrical solution Michael came up with was to use a red, rotating light, like a police car cherry, to set the audience in the right location. Kenny used the overdrive effect on his guitar, playing a low string before jamming his guitar into the speaker of his amp at full volume, so the sound would keep going around in waves, creating a rock and roll imitation of a police car siren, a vital contribution to Michael's perfect application of theater craft, taut and smart, to create the sense of two locations within our single setting. My contribution to all that was "Hey, Kenny, can you come up with a siren sound?"

Between Michael and me, with his large cuts and my trims and edits, we probably cut twenty five minutes or so off the first act after Jonathan passed, but more importantly, we fixed and tightened the outstanding pacing issues. The amazing part of it all was that Jonathan had left us everything, a treasure map of great work that we just had to figure out how to decode. "Here it is," I could hear him saying. "Everything you'll need." At that point I hoped, but as time went on, I *knew*, we had done our best by him. We treated his work with as much professional respect and personal integrity as we could. Jim was right when he said that we knew Jonathan's work better than anyone else. I've always believed Jonathan couldn't have left his work in better hands.

During previews, Michael continued, after he was done making his bodacious cuts, to hone the storytelling, tone, and rhythm of the first act. A part of his process was trying out every possible permutation of the songs "On the Street," "Santa Fe," "I'll Cover You," and "We're Okay." Those songs came right in the middle of act one, three of them with a similar feel and tempo, and it was important that he not let that part of the act sag. Four songs, twelve possible options. It wasn't that they were in the wrong order. Michael just wanted to make sure they were in the *right* order. But for a handful of performances, those four songs were in a different order. Michael didn't want to leave any stone unturned. So in addition to everything I was still fixing, I had to run Michael's nightly changes with the band before each preview. All went fine the first three tries. Then on night four, the cast, band, and I went through the same song-switching routine and we were ready to go—everyone except me. I had forgotten to put my music in the right order, so instead of going "Santa Fe," "I'll Cover You," "We're Okay," I went "Santa Fe," "We're Okay," "I'll Cover You." Unfortunately, since "We're Okay" began with my organ solo, once I started playing there was no way to bail. I had committed everyone—the band, Fredi, the lighting and sound folks, the stage manager—to the wrong sequencing of songs. As I was playing the intro I heard the band shuffling their music and I thought, *Oh no, I've messed it all up,!* and there was no turning back. Was I overloaded, overtired, a little brain-fatigued? Sure I was, but so was everyone else. Thankfully, no one was physically hurt. After that, to my great satisfaction and relief, Michael told me he had decided the order of those four songs, so, mercifully, that was behind us.

As we moved through "Christmas Bells," "Over the Moon," and our freshly cut, remade versions of "La Vie Boheme" and "I Should Tell You," we felt that we'd accomplished everything that we could have possibly done in service to the first act. Still, there was always the lingering question in our minds: did we do enough to get the audience to come back for act two? We were reassured when we saw the audience return to their seats after intermission. The few who had left had gone during the first act, either because the volume of the show was earsplitting or because they saw men kissing men or women kissing women. For everyone who came back to their seats, they knew they had made the right decision when the opening chords of "Seasons of Love" washed over them.

The second act didn't have nearly as many issues as the first act. Even since 1994 the second act had always been sleeker, and in the places where the songs weren't right, Jonathan had fixed them all with his spectacular cuts and rewrites. Sure, there was a little trimming to be done, a few bars here and there that we cut or edited, but again Jonathan had left us with everything we needed. I thought Michael directed Jonathan's work with incredible sensitivity, treating all the life-changing moments for the characters with grace and clarity. There were so many, from Mimi's cheating on Roger with Benny, to Maureen and Joanne's breakup (then makeup. Then breakup reprise. A hot mess), to Angel and Roger's hospitalizations while Mimi's health deteriorated, then Angel's death and memorial, to Mark's meltdown, the seemingly permanent destruction of lifelong friendships, and Roger's plan to leave Mimi and everyone else behind. All of which led to "What You Own," which for all of us came with its own unique baggage. That moment in tech when Jonathan had first passed out three weeks prior was always front of mind. It was all so fraught, overflowing with such emotionally big-ticket, real life-and-death consequences. Michael and the cast negotiated all of it in ways I marveled at.

Musically I made it a point to pare down the orchestrations throughout the second act, saving our loudest, fullest rock versions of ourselves for a few specific moments: the splintering of the group when they emerge from Angel's memorial in "Goodbye Love" and of course "What You Own," when the stakes are at their highest for Mark and Roger simultaneously, even though they were twenty-five hundred miles apart. In act two we made sure there was always someone *not* playing, except in those two songs and "Finale B." I mean, it *is* the finale, right? After we had done all we could do, it was time to roll out the *Rent* carpet.

During previews our show had received a little more attention than it deserved due to Jonathan's unexpected passing. I think there were a lot of curiosity seekers and maybe some people who weren't so well intentioned—the schadenfreude thing and all. There were a lot of people spreading conspiracies that Jonathan was gay and had died from AIDS. This wasn't a surprise since LGBTQ+ identities and the devastating effects of

AIDS were a central theme of his show. But we knew the truth, and what audiences found out was what we all had hoped they would discover—that *Rent* was a masterwork by a revolutionary songwriter with an original vision, a show based on traditional contemporary musical theater traditions, yet told through its creator's thoroughly one-of-a-kind voice. It wasn't long before word started to spread for all the right reasons. We were mostly selling out our previews as word of mouth got out, and the reception grew more enthusiastic night by night as we prowled our way through those two hyper-focused, hyper-vigilant, and incredibly inspiring, grief-stricken weeks. Our work, everything we went through, with purpose and conviction, pointed toward the arrival of the critics, who would show up as they traditionally did, and who would have an outsize say in determining our fate. In other words, were we done or would our show run?

The opening night of a musical is only a celebration of the work that preceded it. The prior three to six previews are known as critics' performances, where press can see the show in order to have their reviews published or broadcast the day after opening night. It's a tradition dating back decades in New York's theater history. Some lesser publications would show up on opening night and even days after, but the ones that matter, the ones that can make or break a new work, come throughout the week before opening. As a courtesy, the paper or magazine usually lets the producers know when they're coming. It's a long-established, tacit agreement that existed between all parties, a kind of rare congeniality and decency in the theater.

The last time I'd had any contact with Jonathan was during one of the critics' performances. It was the weekend prior to the February 13 opening, which fell on a Tuesday night. The *New York Times*'s leading theater critic, Ben Brantley, would be in attendance, and I knew it. Not everyone knew or wanted to know when critics were coming. The *Times* was still, by far, the most influential voice in musical theater, and Mr. Brantley was the tip of the spear. By that week in February, pretty much all of us had gotten over our initial bout of that winter's flu and the show had gained steam and a renewed vitality just in time for the critics. Everything timed out kind of miraculously.

During the Saturday night performance that Brantley attended, we were cruising through act one. We had arrived at "Another Day," the real rocker that Jonathan had written for Roger and Mimi, with the support group joining in toward the end of the song. It was during Mimi's first solo as she sang,

> The heart may freeze, or it can burn
> The pain will ease if I can learn.
> There is no future. There is no past.
> I live in this moment as my last.

I thought, *Please, can you give this guy a break? I mean, he fucking gave his life for this show! Please give him a good review. At least throw him a bone.* Right after silently pleading my case, I felt a cool breeze that gently swept across my face and hair. It wasn't the air-conditioning because it was a cold winter night in February. I knew in my heart what it was, and after that moment passed, I was content, peaceful, and surprisingly relaxed. I truly felt that it had been Jonathan reassuring me, *Don't worry, everything's going to work out fine.* I would have sworn to that under oath.

And sure enough, everything went as Jonathan "said" it would. We had a great, celebratory opening night performance, and the next day multiple reviews came out, all of them positive. Not every critic liked everything, but the consistent themes were Jonathan's incredible score and the kinetic energy of the performers and their performances. Even though the band wasn't singled out in most cases, I think the musical energy was part of the whole potent, dynamic package that was described in many of those reviews.

After the first wave of reviews were out, it all got pretty insane for the Workshop, whose job instantly became dealing with a nonstop stream of calls to their tiny box office phone bank. NYTW had no affiliation with Ticketmaster, which even back then was the leading ticket-selling hub of theater and concert events, so their small staff was managing all interested attendees. According to Jim Nicola, they sold around $30,000 worth of tickets that Wednesday, the day many of those reviews came out, particularly because of the heavily influential *New York Times* piece. Brantley had given Jonathan and the show a glowing review, even by his own uncompromising standards. The Workshop's phones kept ringing, and tickets kept on selling until, in a matter of days, our entire projected run had been completely sold out.

On the bandstand at the Nederlander, 1996. I loved that blue chenille shirt. Thank you, Angela Wendt.

THE TRANSITION
February 14–April 1996

THE GLOW OF GOOD REVIEWS and the show's instant popularity came as a welcome antidote to the weeks that preceded the opening. The task of putting in Michael's carefully considered changes had exerted a hard physical and emotional toll no one could have anticipated. When the public and critical response to everyone's effort was so immensely enthusiastic, we collectively exhaled. Finally the pressure valve had been released, so the cast had more fun doing their work.

Soon after we opened, Michael had to go back to his job at the La Jolla Playhouse and the rest of us kept rolling, eight shows a week, through the end of February and into the beginning of March 1996. Without an associate musical director to play for me while I sat in the audience and took notes once a week, Jim and Michael asked how we would keep the quality control of the music at an optimal level. I volunteered to take home a recording of each performance, listen to the show and compile notes, then distribute them accordingly. I did as promised, but I also took notes in my head during each act and wrote them down at intermission and after the show while they were still fresh. It only took me a week to figure out that what I was hearing onstage every night from the cast and band was the same as what the recordings were telling me. I kept up that routine for a couple weeks, and once I was absolutely convinced that my notetaking was solid, I stopped, with Michael's and Jim's blessing.

As word of the show spread, especially among the entertainment community, it seemed that everyone wanted to come. The band and I started to notice the celebs not long after we opened, even if, because we still had to pack up and store our gear, we only sort of noticed them. It wasn't a subject of conversation between us—obviously they were there to see the cast—but I do particularly remember a few icons. Among them, Diane Sawyer, who I remember being there a lot because at the time she was married to Mike Nichols, who had helped Cy O'Neal with the founding of Friends In Deed; also Danny DeVito and Rhea Perlman; and I absolutely noticed the singers Joe Jackson ("Steppin' Out") and Ric Ocasek (lead singer of The Cars) because they were both incredibly tall. Ocasek had his signature shock of onyx black hair, Jackson his perfectly clean-shaven head. Since the theater's only exit was through the house, the cast had to come out of their dressing rooms and cross downstage to the stairs, which meant they always passed a hodgepodge of celebrities and other folks waiting on or near the stage. It was informal and cool, like your family and friends looking forward to seeing you as soon as they could. It became, in a way, the show after the show. For our exhausted yet exuberant cast, it must have been hugely exciting. They went from complete unknowns to people everyone wanted to meet, hug, talk with, and congratulate. All in less than a week.

During previews, as we knew the show was getting pretty good, we started wondering if *Rent* had a life beyond NYTW. After the reviews came out, those conversations got real. Since our commercial producers, Kevin and Jeffrey, were on board, they would have the final say-so about the show's future. There was a former TV studio a block up from NYTW, on East Fifth Street just off Bowery, that had been vacant for a while. It was a large space where a lot of live television had been shot from the 1950s through the 1970s. Kevin and Jeffrey had considered converting that space into a hybrid theater-nightclub where *Rent* could perform its eight shows per week. I heard a little chatter about moving the show into a church on East Ninth Street, as well as another vacated space farther south in the East Village, but nothing concrete. For Jim any of those settings would have been ideal, fulfilling his dream of having a successful show celebrating the East Village realized and running in the neighborhood.

The band, however, was on a completely different track. We were the definitive armchair producers. Sure, we cared about the show, but what we really cared about was consistent, decent-paying work. I looked at the pay scales for the Minetta Lane Theatre, a well-known off-Broadway theater in the West Village that would be able to house our show. Eight shows, $710 per week. Now we were talkin'! We all thought it would be great if we could finish the run at the Workshop, then move into Minetta Lane for the summer. My one-liner to the band had to be altered to "Stick with me and you'll make in the mid-to-*high* three figures." We opined that, of course, our show couldn't move to Broadway. The cast was too big (it wasn't), the show wasn't a traditional Broadway show for traditional Broadway audiences (possibly true), and besides, what if we aimed too high, got out over our skis, and failed? We'd be out of work. If they'd only listen to us. We all thought we knew something, but we didn't know squat. We were five grandmothers sitting around the bandstand, knitting needles in hand, talking about the world of commercial Broadway production.

Traditionally on the morning the *New York Times*, *New York Post*, and *Daily News* came out (the three most widely published dailies in New York at the time, as well as *Daily Variety*, the definitive entertainment business publication for the East and West

Coast entertainment industries), a show's commercial producers would meet with their advertising, marketing, and publicity teams to develop a strategy that, based on that morning's reviews, would promote the show in the best way possible. Did they have the strength, momentum, budget, and guts to move a new show up the ladder and on to a larger-capacity theater? For the *Rent* team, the big question was whether they could move it, and if so, where they could best capitalize on the enthusiasm around the show so it would become profitable.

Everyone who attended that meeting knew what they were seeing. They had been to multiple previews and had heard our enthusiastic audiences. After some discussion, Jeffrey stood up and took the leap. "We're moving to Broadway!" he declared. And that was it. No one disagreed. Kevin and Jeffrey had an audacious plan. Not only would the show move to Broadway, but it would move quickly and during the spring theater season, in time for the Obie and Tony Award nominations. Strike while the show was hot. The news got down to us quickly, within a day or so, and in the interim, based on the crazy ticket sales, NYTW announced a two-week extension of our run. The band was happy with the two extra weeks of work. None of us had any delusions about a lengthy, successful Broadway run, I think mostly because we didn't want to get our hopes up. Musician's instinct. Don't count on work that isn't guaranteed. There was no union contract that promised a year's work, much less six months. We had a simple "run of show" agreement. The musicians would get paid until the show closed, no severance, nada.

In the early part of March, we went theater shopping a few hours a day. I was grateful that Kevin, Jeffrey, and Michael, who was back on the East Coast for a few weeks, invited me along on those shopping trips. I felt like a real valued member of the team, even though I had no say in any of the decision-making. We looked at a handful of theaters over the course of a week or so, in various states of habitability. Some were established theaters ready for occupancy, some needed repair, and a couple were in the middle of full-on reconstruction. It was great to be shown theaters whose owners or landlords wanted our show. The coolest part for me was when we entered each theater and I felt like we were being shown what might be our future, for however long. We went to the Lyceum Theatre, which especially stuck out in my mind because that's where I first saw Whoopi Goldberg's one-woman show in 1985. I hadn't been there since, but I had remembered the upstage center entrance, which would have fit our show beautifully. It was snug as Broadway theaters go, seating just under a thousand people, and very tall (I had sat in the second mezzanine back in 1985, and that was four floors up), but because its audience capacity was limited by Broadway standards, it had a smaller, more intimate playing space. Paul Clay certainly could have redesigned the sculpture, which might have made the bandstand/support group platform a little tighter, but it wasn't ever going to be perfect. Still, I was a little disappointed when Kevin and Jeffrey rejected it out of hand. I also remember looking at the Martin Beck Theatre, a truly magnificent, big, modern Broadway theater, with a capacity of over fourteen hundred, that looked gigantic compared to the Lyceum. Everyone tacitly agreed that the Martin Beck was too modern and potentially too big for us. I felt there wasn't much soul to it.

Under the category of theaters under construction, we visited the Selwyn Theatre on West Forty-Second Street. It had been gutted and when we looked at its renovation in real time, it seemed kind of cool and appropriate. Unlike the Martin Beck, the Selwyn had some edge to it. It had been a grindhouse theater that ran low budget, second-rate, adult-only films, twenty-four seven. It was part of Forty-Second Street's row of sleazy, seedy theaters and porn houses from the sixties until the early nineties. That seemed like a pretty good history for a theater that we might move into.

But the timetable of the reconstruction didn't fit Kevin and Jeffrey's schedule.

We eventually made our way to the Nederlander Theatre. Although it had a rich and storied history dating back to the twenties, it was going through a rough stretch at the time of our visit, one that had been fifteen years in the making. It hadn't had any long runs of Broadway shows since 1981 with *Lena Horne: The Lady and Her Music*, which ran for a little more than a year. Aside from that, there were short runs of plays and concerts until 1992, when there had been a little bit of anticipation for a Rupert Holmes play, *Solitary Confinement*, starring Stacy Keach. It ran for a month.

Since the Nederlander was located on West Forty-First Street, it wasn't considered part of Times Square and, as a result, not a "real" part of the Broadway Theater District. Consequently, it had fallen slowly, inevitably, into disrepair after the Lena Horne show, with a minor facelift for Stacy Keach. By the time we got there in 1996, there hadn't been a single occupant for four years. The roof of the theater was leaking, not just in one place, and it was cold in a damp, bone-chilling way. I could feel the mold crawling into my skin when we walked into the place. Nope, no shortage of funk in there. Yet despite its condition, it was off the beaten path, like the Workshop, and also wasn't in the best part of town. The stage itself could have been a replica of our stage at the Workshop (with bigger wing and backstage space). Most importantly though, the Nederlanders were ready for us to move in immediately. That fit Kevin and Jeffrey's plan. We had found our new home. It was a fixer-upper, but it was a home.

Meanwhile, back downtown, we were purring along through our two-week extension to our last performance on Sunday, March 31. We were crushing it, show after show. The strength, fortitude, and resolve of that company during those two months going back to Jonathan's death were incredible. Everyone was sick at some point, but no one called out. The show wouldn't relent to weather or germs.

For the cast and the rest of us, help was on the way. Since we would be moving to Broadway, we would finally be able to hire understudies. Michael, Bernie, Marlies and I spent part of March auditioning the newest members of our growing family. It wasn't too difficult casting them because two of the six understudies had been with us previously. Mark Setlock and Shelley Dickinson were both in the 1994 production, Yassmin Alers had done another of Jonathan's shows (called *Blocks*) with Anthony and Rodney, and her sister, Karmine, had done *Rent*'s 1993 reading, so she was as *Rent*-adjacent as one could be. Since we had to have at least two understudies for all fifteen roles (the rest would come from within the current cast), the six we hired had to be versatile and get up to speed. Fast. The other three understudies we hired fit that bill perfectly: Darius de Haas, David Driver, and Simone (her real name was Lisa Simone, and she was the daughter of the legendary singer, songwriter, pianist and activist, Nina Simone), We were now twenty-one strong in the cast, with three stage managers instead of two, along with our Nederlander crew who we'd meet soon enough.

In addition to casting the understudies, we had some brush-up rehearsals at NYTW during the last two weeks of March, and I spent that time ordering keyboards and amps for our impending move. I was entrusted with upgrading the gear as I saw fit. There were no hard budgetary restrictions given to me; our producers and general management knew that I'd spend responsibly. Music gear was easy to come by, so there was no time crunch even if we ordered stuff directly from the manufacturer, which we did in a couple cases. Everyone in the band was thrilled. It was rare for the five of us to be told, "Get whatever you want within reason and you get to decide what's within reason."

First I asked Kenny what he wanted as far as a guitar amp

was concerned. He had used his own Music Man amp for the downtown run, but now he had a much wider range of choices to consider. He could pick the best amp that would go along with his guitars of choice. He, like so many guitar players, had an extensive personal collection, so he continually swapped guitars in and out of the show until he found his best guitar-amp combo. He ended up buying his own amp and guitar head, because he wanted to own that model anyway. He bought a Rivera speaker cabinet and a guitar head called the Rivera Knuckle Head '55. What's better than a manufacturer with a sense of humor? As for Dan, he was cool with his guitars, but his downtown amp was an old Fender Blues Deluxe which no longer sounded good. When we moved uptown, he upgraded substantially to a VHT Pitbull 45. So with Dan's Korg CX-3 organ and its new sidekick, a mini replica of a Leslie organ cabinet from a company called Motion Sound that I'd discovered, and the Kurzweil keyboard, he was good to go. I got a Kurzweil as well, and a few other rack-mounted keyboards to add flavor to the layered keyboard sounds I had in my imagination. Steph was cool. She didn't need an amp because she would be going directly from the output of her bass into an ultra-high-end preamp called the Avalon U5, then to the mixing console. Jeff was happy with his setup, so he brought his drum kit and electronic drum rig uptown. During those two weeks while Michael, the cast, and I were rehearsing, I was mostly consumed by musical retail therapy or, as I thought of it, gear porn.

At the beginning of April we moved uptown to the Nederlander, where we would reconfigure our spacing, lighting, and mount our show for its Broadway debut, beginning with previews on the sixteenth of that month. As amped up as we all were about the move, none of the band talked about our Broadway future specifically. I think we were a little stunned by what was happening. Jeff was the only band member who was there from 1994, and on occasion he'd say to me, "Look what's happened to our little show." He said it when the reviews came out, when we sold out our run downtown, when it was announced where and when we were moving, and the day the band brought their gear to the Nederlander. The first few days in our new home brought an unexpected sense of familiarity alongside the we're-not-in-Kansas-anymore feeling.

The best part of the Nederlander was that its playing space was eerily similar to the one at NYTW. The Workshop, which only had 199 seats, had a full-on proscenium stage, measuring roughly forty-six feet wide by thirty-one feet deep—gigantic for a nonprofit, off-Broadway theater. The square footage of the stage was outsize compared to the audience seating area. Most theaters, to maximize their earning potential, would have a smaller stage area to accommodate a larger paying audience. That was part of the Workshop's appeal in comparison to other theaters. The size of the stage mattered because it gave flexibility to a show's cast and crew. That was in line with the Workshop's principles, and a show like ours benefitted from it, with our cast of fifteen and our five-piece onstage band.

How great was it, then, when we got into the Nederlander to find that the width of the stage was forty feet and the depth was thirty feet, plus four feet of playing space below the proscenium if we needed it? Michael, Kevin, and Jeffrey had talked through the appeal of this setup before we landed there, but when the rest of the company first saw the stage, they were struck by its familiarity, even though they'd never been there. We all knew essentially what we were dealing with coming in, which made a move full of other unknowns much easier. And we would be met with comforts of the old stage as well: Paul Clay had brought the junk sculpture up from downtown, as well as the band platform, and the coolest thing he did was to re-create the Workshop's azure blue brick wall with a graffitied drop curtain thirty feet upstage so that everything on stage looked almost exactly like it had downtown. It felt like we had teleported from East Fourth Street to West Forty-First Street.

While Michael, Marlies, and Blake were all reconfiguring the show on our new stage, I kept busy programming the new gear I had bought for our uptown move. Because I had been buying and programming synthesizers since the seventies, I prided myself on the fact that I could get into any synth and in a pretty short amount of time figure out how it worked and what the similarities and differences were from manufacturer to manufacturer. It was fun work to me that never felt tedious, only creative and rewarding. As I learned the inner workings of each new piece of gear, and with the universality of MIDI, I created sounds that were a real step up from what I had been able to make downtown on my older and less versatile setup. The whole process—figuring out how the new gear worked, then coming up with more complex sounds—was kind of nerdy but highly enjoyable. I needed to wear headphones for that work, and the privacy it afforded me was a bonus, especially with so much activity swirling around me.

Besides our work onstage, there was the work going on in the building itself. Every Broadway theater has its own in-house crew. From carpenters, electricians, plumbers, riggers, and painters to property (prop) people, spotlight operators, and special effects people—anything a show needs, they manage. We didn't know them when we arrived, but we soon learned how invaluable they were to our process and hopefully to our success. They were highly skilled professionals, capable of accomplishing anything that was needed. A crew knows its theater and its idiosyncrasies inside and out. No matter the peculiarities of each individual house, the crews keep everything humming. Our new collaborators made the entire theater comfortable for us and habitable for audiences, despite the tight six-week window they had to make it happen. Joe, Billy Wright, Billy Jr., Jan, Morgan, and the rest were very welcoming while managing the incredible amount of work they had to do. From fixing ceilings to repairing plumbing in the dressing rooms, no job was too big or too insignificant. We learned from the get-go that we were guests in their house, like college exchange students staying with a host family, only in our case we hoped to be there long past a semester.

Due to the harsh winter that was still hanging around, lingering into the early spring, the theater was in rough shape. There was a ton of leakage coming into the theater as the winter's snowpack finally relented and began to melt. The most noticeable gash was a huge hole in the back left corner of the upper mezzanine, which allowed water to drip down onto the seats, floors, and carpets. The drenched seats couldn't be replaced until the melting stopped, and the drying and repainting of all the damaged areas were a big job. There was cold and mold everywhere, so the heat wasn't too effective for the first week or so after we started rehearsing, but the crew was all over that as well. Still, at the beginning stages, it was just nasty all around. I was happy that the band wasn't scheduled to come in yet, because the guitars and basses, whose necks were wooden, would have warped from the dampness and cold temperatures. Damage to those instruments' bodies, particularly the necks and electrical components, could have rendered them unplayable. Expensive and in some cases one-of-a-kind creations would have been destroyed. We had cheaper, replaceable electric and acoustic guitars for Roger to play live, which we needed during rehearsals. They too got pretty beat up during that time, as I expected. Instead of buying new ones, we got all of them fully repaired and set up again before we went into previews. It was the cheaper option, so we took it. We were still, in those small financial ways, cautious.

Every department had upgrading to do. On the set design side, the new back "wall" had to be painted to mimic the Workshop's wall, and Paul added a little more graffiti to it for the uptown version. He also built out his iconic junk sculpture a bit, as well as the Christmas lights and decorations around the upstage left bandstand and the platform above it, which served as the home of the Life Support group. I never got sick of looking at the junk sculpture. I always discovered something new: a clown mask, a bicycle tire, a teddy bear with one eye ripped out. It was an incredibly well composed installation that injected the set, like the heroin of its time, with a late-eighties post-punk vitality. What I recognized most was how the sculpture created light and shadows. I figured if I could notice it, it was quite noticeable. I had great ears, not a great eye. And on top of it all, as Paul had conceived it two years prior, it was an entirely functional set piece, despite its junkiness. There were plenty of places on which to sit, walk through, perch, stand, hang, and swing.

Angela got more of a costume budget to work with when we moved uptown, but all I knew about the clothing in the theater was that I was very comfy in my soft and cozy blue chenille shirt with its three-quarter sleeves, my oversize black sweatpants, and my black sneakers. It felt great, and the loose clothing helped me to play and conduct freely. All our designers and creators—Paul, Blake, Marlies, and Angela—did such incredibly creative and tasteful work, at least as I saw it. They all made it look impossibly simple, and their pursuit of Jonathan's vision, through Michael's guidance and their own creativity, was incredible to behold as it took shape. They had truly imagined and realized a world within a world, and it was laid bare before our audiences when they walked in.

As people came through the front doors, past the box office, they were treated to downtown artwork by downtown artists lining the foyer. Paul wanted to showcase the work of East Village artists, just as his junk sculpture reflected similar East Village installations in the 1980s by the artists of the Rivington School. Our audiences were immediately brought into a world that I had recently moved into and had come to cherish. I'd never before felt so comfortable or at home in any theater I had worked in. It was more than a place to go to work. I already felt like I belonged there.

Cold, clammy rehearsals continued as the crew brought the Nederlander back to life. I remember coming in after a Sunday off, and as I walked into the theater all layered up for another week of rehearsal, I discovered that, whoa, it was warmer! I peeled off a layer or two, looked toward the upper left corner of the balcony, and saw that the hole in the ceiling had been plastered and painted. That crew did what they had to do, from the time they found out we were moving in there all the way through previews and until opening night and beyond. Superhuman to me, but for them just another day at the office.

Besides all the insanity from our opening downtown in February to our rehearsal and tech period at the Nederlander in April, my life had been upended in ways that were, frankly, unexpected, amazing, and beautiful, in an entirely different way than the show was unexpected, amazing, and beautiful. My first marriage had fizzled out and I was learning way too much about the divorce laws in New York. In March my friend Lonny was hosting his birthday party and told me that following a lot of thought, he was inviting a friend of his so I could meet her. The friend was the Broadway actress Randy Graff, who was in the show *Moon Over Buffalo* and was coming up to Lon's after a matinee and evening performance, unaware she was walking into a loose fix-up. Since we were still downtown, I didn't arrive at Lonny's Upper West Side apartment until well past eleven, by which point Lonny had told Randy that he had a friend who he thought might be a good match and the guy was coming up after his show was over. Randy, who looked more like she was going camping than to a party, the consequence of a two-show day, said, "Where's my lipstick?"

to which Lonny replied, "Not for this one." He knew me so well. I did eventually get uptown to Lon's apartment and met Randy. We spoke for barely more than a few minutes, just party chitchat, and I told her I'd call. Later she told me that with her cynical view of the dating world, she'd thought, *Yeah, right.*

I did call though, and our first date was at a quiet restaurant called the World Café. Nothing worldly about it. Just another overpriced restaurant on Columbus Avenue. Since we were both working, the best option was lunch. I'm sure that was how the first date of many showbiz relationships began. It was all about scheduling. Our tacit understanding was let's eat, get to know each other a little, then get on with our days. She walked in, and besides confirming how cute I'd thought she was, I noticed she was wearing blue suede shoes. Whether or not that was an Elvis-inspired choice, I didn't know, but I liked them.

Before Lon's party I'd known Randy in name only. I couldn't have picked her out of a lineup. I had heard her on the *City of Angels* original cast recording and my first thought wasn't about her voice, great as it was, but her time. Old-school, Capitol Records time. Frank Sinatra and Nelson Riddle time with a side of Rosemary Clooney and Anita O'Day. Who was this Broadway singer who could really swing? We didn't talk a lot about work, but we both were aware of what each other was doing. The slightly awkward moment that first date came when we spoke generally about our pasts and careers. I told her about mine, pretty much all downtown or out of town (except for my Broadway flop with Joan Rivers and subbing), and as Randy told me about the shows she had done, she mentioned *Les Misérables*. My response to that was "Oh, you were in that? I really liked Colm Wilkinson. I thought the song 'Bring Him Home' was beautiful." Randy looked at me quizzically and said, "You don't remember Fantine? 'I Dreamed a Dream'?" I thought about it for a second, then replied, "No, I don't." That

MAKING RENT

(167)

unfortunate exchange reaffirmed that I was truly from off the Broadway farm.

All in all, we had a nice first date, despite the "*Les Mis* incident." There was a bit of electricity in the air. I paid for lunch in the old-fashioned, traditional man way and in the process spent almost half of all the money I had in the world. Lunch was $35, and my bank account said $78 and change.

A few weeks later I walked Randy to her theater in Midtown and she brought me in to meet her stage manager and the star of her play, Carol Burnett. Randy and Carol had become good friends by then and Carol wanted to check me out to see if I was worthy. Randy introduced us, but instead of making the usual small talk, Carol immediately pulled up my lips to get a look at my teeth and gums. She looked inside my mouth as if she were buying a horse. She (shamelessly) brought the element of surprise to our introduction, and yes, it was hilarious, but I couldn't laugh so easily with someone's thumbs in my mouth. I guess my orthodonture passed the test because Randy didn't break up with me after her show that night.

My overall disposition became sunnier with Randy in my life. I knew that after our shows were done and we were back home, the night would end with us talking on the phone instead of me going to an Irish bar for a pint and a shot and then back to my dreary, grimy apartment. I remembered how depressing the winter after Jonathan's death had been, and although I was still carrying around that heavy stone in my pocket, Randy and I were starting to find our groove. As Jonathan wrote in "La Vie Boheme": "to passion, when it's new."

At last our show was cruising toward previews, and the late-winter temperatures were rising. There were many late afternoons, and on the weekends many late mornings, when I'd walk Randy down to her theater on West Forty-Fifth Street and then continue down to the Nederlander on West Forty-First

Street. Even though our theaters were only four blocks away from each other, going below Forty-Second Street felt like a shift to another time. Even in the mid-nineties our block still resembled the New York of the late seventies and eighties. Compared to the theater where Randy was working, the Martin Beck (which we had looked at for our show about a month earlier), we were mounting our show in a dumpster. Part of me thought, *Sure, we built it, but will people come?* It was one thing for 199 people to come to the groovy New York Theatre Workshop, but would that translate uptown?

We had been in tech since Wednesday, April 10, and had previews beginning the following Tuesday. All the creatives, me included, had done most of what we had to do prior to tech. It was, as I had been told, a relatively easy transfer from downtown. Most shows took at least six weeks or so to get on their Broadway footing, but be we were already fully formed, our show spent only a week in rehearsal and a week in tech before going into previews, with the opening just under two weeks later.

While we were in the second week of rehearsal, our producers and some strangers showed up at the back of the theater, and Michael announced over his mic, "Let's take a break, everyone." The last time Michael had announced an unscheduled break, Jonathan had been on the floor at the back of the Workshop's theater with EMTs hovering over him. This time, in some unbelievably twisted but beautifully poetic kind of way, the shock from the back of the theater came as our producers, Kevin and Jeffrey, declared, "Jonathan Larson has just won the Pulitzer Prize for Drama!" At this everyone broke into thunderous applause, smiling, cheering, and hugging. I, however, stayed by myself, in my chair behind the keyboard, trying to make sense of it all. It was awesome news, obviously, but here we were again celebrating without Jonathan there to revel in his achievement. I was happy it would bring some joy to his family, Jim and the other folks at

NYTW, and all of us who had helped bring the show across the finish line, but I had a hard time wrapping my mind around it. I'd already known Jonathan's work was special, even if I'd never thought of it in terms of a Pulitzer Prize.

The outro to Earth, Wind & Fire's 1976 hit, "Can't Hide Love," begins at the song's 2:11 mark. Its underlying accompaniment is a descending chromatic succession of chords, beginning with E♭/F, then D/E, to D♭/E♭, and so on, until you get to A/B. The vocals on top of those chords are "Ahhs" in three phrases. The last note is a beautiful A-major chord held for two beats. Angelic and gorgeous, and then the entire sequence repeats until the song fades out.

Late one night during the second week of tech, close to 11:30 p.m., after a third straight day that had begun at noon, the cast was sitting and standing in their final tableau for "Will I?" and I was at the piano. Everyone had to stay on their marks so Blake could light them properly, the last event of a long and harrowing day. We had been through an intense time in the days prior, working through the technically challenging first act just as we had downtown, only now we were in a larger theater with our new crew. We were all eager to get out of the theater and go home, with one more cue to button up the preceding twelve hours, and for Blake this was no small task, especially now with a bigger lighting package to deploy. He was working on a delicate moment in the show and had to get it exactly right. Considering how much of a grind that day had been, I was amazed how everyone quietly stayed in their places. They were all just dog-tired.

In that moment, my sometimes-annoying habit of noodling on the piano in the quiet of tech made another appearance, just as it had when we were downtown. For no apparent reason I started softly playing the outro chords to "Can't Hide Love." Slowly, gradually, one person joined in, then another one, then two more, then three, then four, until the entire cast came in, singing that gorgeous outro in octaves, just like on the record. The men sang on the bottom and the women sang an octave higher. But when we got to the last beautiful A-major chord, the men jumped up the octave (mostly singing in falsetto) to make it sound exactly like it did on the record. Since they were so tired, they sang it softly and exquisitely, like an R & B hymn. This went on for a little while, like a cool-down to an aerobics class. I think we made it through around four or five passes before Michael got on his mic and said, "Thank you everybody. See you tomorrow." At that, the piano and I melted away and the vocals stopped, but the vibe stayed in the air. I said to no one and everyone, "I bet they're not doing that over at *State Fair*."

Curtain call, opening night at the Nederlander Theatre, April 29, 1996.

LIFTOFF
Spring–Summer 1996

RENT'S OPENING NIGHT ON BROADWAY was April 29, 1996—a Monday, which was an unusual night of the week to open a show. Most new shows wanted to open on a Thursday night, so the reviews would come out in the major publications on Friday, when readership was higher. If there was no room on a Thursday (newspapers and magazines only have so many critics to assign to shows), they'd try to open on Wednesday, and on Tuesday if they had no choice. But Monday? Nothing to worry about, Kevin and Jeffrey told me. I figured they had very reassuring intel, so it didn't matter what night we opened.

The band, as usual, came out to our places a few minutes before the start of the show. We'd get tuned up, put on our headphones, make sure everything was where it should be, and go through whatever else we did before a gig. Casual and professional. But when we came out opening night, the audience went nuts. When the cast entered, they went berserk! I felt the audience's reaction to my core; it was rooted in love, appreciation, and a deep understanding of our journey. There was a two- or three-minute standing ovation before the show even began. Then Anthony Rapp, the first person cast in 1994, came downstage.

"We dedicate this and every performance to the memory of Jonathan Larson," he declared, his voice engaging and purposeful. Another long ovation followed.

That performance was the ultimate collision of everything celebratory and unfair about the whole situation. The deep sadness and the exuberance; the despair and the satisfaction of our accomplishment; Jonathan's unfathomable death and our relentless commitment to him. The affection we received from the audience that night allowed us to put our mourning of Jonathan into a safe and secure place in our hearts once and for all. From that point on we shared and honored Jonathan's magnum opus unabashedly with everyone who came to see the show in our new uptown home.

The rest of that week was more of the same. Audiences going wild for the show. All twenty of us on that stage were as one. As unified in purpose, execution, spirit, and togetherness as anything I had ever been a part of in my professional life. The reviews came out in droves beginning the day after our opening. In local print media, we were reviewed by the *New York Post*, the *New York Daily News*, and the *New York Times*. On local TV, channels two, four, seven, nine, and eleven gave coverage as well. Reviews in national publications included *Time*, *Newsweek*, *Variety*, *Entertainment Weekly*, *People*, and many more. The *Times* did a feature on the entire cast with individual photos and bios of *all fifteen* of them. I'd never seen anything like that. We did all the television shows: David Letterman, Jay Leno (for which we all got flown out—cast and band—to Los Angeles on a Monday morning, did the taping, then flew back, crashed, and were ready to roll on Tuesday), the *Rosie O'Donnell Show*, the *Today* show, *Good Morning America*, and more—it seemed like the entire morning and evening lineup. Our demand was so extreme, we probably could have sung on *Wheel of Fortune*. Later that summer, we were flown out to Chicago's United Center to sing at the Democratic National Convention, the year of then-President Bill Clinton's reelection (the Clintons came to the show twice—once as a regular family outing and the other as a celebration of Chelsea's birthday, with Chelsea's friends in tow). After opening night and all the television appearances, there was a natural crashing effect, as some of the cast members' bodies and voices started to break down to varying degrees. Amazingly though, everyone came to work every night. No one wanted to be the first to call out sick. That wouldn't happen for a few more months. It had to come sometime, just not while we were burning down the house every night.

While all those media appearances were happening, I was in the eye of the hurricane. I only knew about the initial wave of reviews and our outside obligations, but that was it. I didn't know what a cultural phenomenon the show was fast becoming, because I was in my own world, in my tiny apartment, stationed at my small table. All my days, when I didn't have to be somewhere else, were spent on the phone, either responding to the "Tim, I need . . ." or "Tim, can you . . ." requests and feverishly writing out the score by hand. The band parts were still unfinished. Everyone's music was the result of updating our books as we went, through rehearsal, previews, and performances downtown (I had told them during rehearsals that the books wouldn't be finished until they were finished). Even through our early weeks on Broadway they weren't completely clean, but they were legible enough for our first round of substitute musicians to navigate. My task was a little tougher. All the work I had done since rehearsal started was either marked up in my rehearsal book or in the score I was using on Broadway, so what I played from every show was a combination of both. The score I was writing out by hand had to include all those changes, but the biggest decisions I had to make were about which versions of Jonathan's melody writing to commit to. Should I go with what Jonathan had written verbatim or with the musical choices that had happened, or were happening, since he'd passed? I was torn, but I erred on the conservative side, preserving much more of Jonathan's work rather than less.

Michael and I had agreed that *Rent* wouldn't be a one-size-fits-all show. Not all plug and play. Just as Jesse had sung differently from Pat, so it was that the next "Seasons of Love" soloist might sing differently from Gwen, and so on. Michael and I would embrace that approach where necessary, always retaining the integrity of Jonathan's score. Also, I knew that some of the group harmonies would change a little over time. It was good but still not perfect. I didn't have enough time to fully write out a separate piano rehearsal book and I regretted that it never got done, but I had deadlines to meet—for the producers, copyists, and musicians' union. It was a complicated set of circumstances, so I had to prioritize as best I could because my free time was so limited. And it was about to become way more limited the following Monday when the *Rent* band would start laying down tracks for the original Broadway cast recording.

On Monday, May 6, the band assembled at Sorcerer Sound Recording Studios in the East Village to lay down some basic tracks without vocals. With help from our crew, all our gear had gone down to Sorcerer first thing Monday morning, and we would pack it up Tuesday to have it brought back to the theater for that night's performance. We arrived early for our 10:00 a.m. start and met everyone who would be involved in the recording from the production side. Amazingly, the legendary Arif Mardin would be producing the album. Even though he had recorded many of my jazz heroes, he was best known for his work with Atlantic Records when the company created its signature R & B "Atlantic Sound" in the 1960s, having worked alongside the great Jerry Wexler, as well as the Ertegun brothers (who, like Arif, were of Turkish descent). Arif produced well over one hundred albums, including Aretha Franklin's *Young, Gifted and Black,* Dusty Springfield's *Dusty in Memphis,* and the Bee Gees' soundtrack to the movie *Saturday Night Fever*. Later in his career he produced Norah Jones's first hit album, *Come Away with Me*. Other artists he had worked with included Hall & Oates, Roberta Flack and Donny Hathaway, Chaka Khan, the Average White Band, and the list goes on. Forever and prolific. Oh yeah, and there were those eleven Grammy Awards. But *Rent* wasn't his first rodeo with Broadway cast recordings. He had produced and won a Grammy for *Smokey Joe's Cafe* just a year prior to *Rent*. It was humbling, to say the least, and a real honor to be in the room with a music legend like Arif. He brought with him his engineer, Mike O'Reilly, and our old friend Steve Skinner, who would be the album's coproducer. Steve had worked as an arranger for Arif on some of Bette Midler's work, and when Arif found out that it was Steve who had produced all of Jonathan's demos, his title and role were a natural fit.

After Mike and his crew got all of us mic'd and cabled up, off we went. First up was "Out Tonight." Very straight-ahead, no stops and starts, and it was nice to come out of the gate rocking in a tempo that was easy first thing in the morning. We did a take or two and then Arif invited us into the control room to have a listen, which was a very kind gesture. Historically, Broadway cast albums were made very quickly, purely due to business decisions (Broadway cast albums rarely recouped their costs), and so musicians normally wouldn't have the luxury of listening to a playback, much less the opportunity to do multiple takes of a song. But this album would be different. Because the show was already wildly popular, our producers had decided to take more time, spend whatever money was necessary and make a great record, not just one day of recording and a day of mixing. We didn't listen to every playback of course, but it was kind of Arif to bring us in to listen to a few. The playbacks we did hear confirmed what we already knew: that the *Rent* band was making high-quality music together. We were listening to each other, playing off one another, and, most importantly, we were playing *freely* in the moment. In every moment really. It had been about five months since we'd started at the Workshop, and by the time we opened on Broadway we had achieved what so many bands chased. As a band we had caught lightning in a bottle, so in the end we only had to do a couple multiple takes.

After recording "Out Tonight," we moved on to "Rent," "Light My Candle," "Today 4 U," and "You'll See." On the original cast recording there is a noticeable edit at the beginning of "You'll See." In the show, after the two-bar intro, Benny would sing, "Joy to the world . . ." and then move on. That bit never made it onto the recording. Jonathan's original entrance for Benny was four bars of Bob Geldof and Midge Ure's 1984 song, "Do They Know It's Christmas?" which mobilized huge amounts of money and visibility for famine relief in Ethiopia. Since the 1994 version of *Rent*, Benny had entered singing the lines, "Feed the world. Let them know it's Christmas time . . ." before "Hey, you bum! Yeah, you! Move over! Get your ass off that Range Rover!" Well, Geldof got wind of this due to *Rent*'s popularity and asked our producers to remove those lyrics from the show. I understood why. In our show those lyrics were used flippantly, merely as a device to get Benny into the scene—it wasn't particularly respectful of the lyric's original intent. Kevin called me one day and said, "Tim, we can't use the 'feed the world' section. Can you find something public domain that we can substitute instead?" So I found what would be the eventual solution, built the piano part so it would sound like what Jonathan would have played, and that's how Benny came to sing, "Joy to the world, the—hey, you bum . . . !" When we were doing the record, it was right in the middle of all that, hence the edit.

The piano I played on at Sorcerer was slightly out of tune and the pedal assembly was broken. I heard it during the playbacks. I didn't whine. Nothing could be done to fix it. Initially, I wasn't happy that "Seasons of Love" was being played on this imperfect piano that was on a lot of the record, but I realized that it would sound more like a piano in an older church in the East Village, a smart choice by Arif in the end.

The next week we moved our recording operations to Midtown Manhattan. We were supposed to have begun there two weeks prior but had been forced to start downtown at the last minute due to a scheduling snafu. We moved into Right Track Studios on West Forty-Eighth Street, music row, where we would continue tracking and laying down all the vocals, and where Arif would eventually mix most of the record (the rest was done at Sony Studios). It had opened there in 1976 and was one of the last holdouts in that area of town before they eventually opened a larger facility farther west, near Tenth Avenue on Thirty-Eighth Street, in the early 2000s.

The vocals began with "Seasons of Love," just like we had done in rehearsals. No one told Arif to do that. It was his own sensibility, good judgment, and taste. The great thing about Right Track was they had lots of square footage in two of their three studios (we recorded in Studio A), so setting up recording booths for a large group of singers was easy. We had fifteen singers split into five booths, nine men in three booths, and six women in the other two. A great template for Arif that made it easy to record and mix that song. That's one of the reasons "Seasons of Love" A and B sound so great on the recording. We finished up those two songs easily and moved on to "Rent." I was kind of amazed that this young cast felt as comfortable as they did in the studio, knowing almost instinctively when to step up for their solos or duets and when to step back and sing together. They slipped into it like a comfortable shoe, as if they'd recorded many times before.

I don't know why Arif decided to record the songs in the order he did, beyond the logical reason to do all the group numbers first instead of piecemeal. Maybe it was instinct, his feeling the energy in the room, or something built on knowledge a legendary producer has that the rest of us don't. For whatever reason, he chose to do "Will I?" next. This was the first song where Arif took advantage of what the recording medium offered, and he had a great idea. He said, "Tim, I'd like to expand this song out a little more." The cast all took a short break while I went into the control room with Arif. He asked, "Can you add another verse for everyone, then over that last verse I'd like you to write a descant for one of the women to sing on top of everyone. Can we try that?"

"Absolutely," I replied.

Rather than have Gwen sing it, which would have been the obvious choice, I went to Fredi. In the show we only heard Fredi sing in her chest voice due to the range that Jonathan had written for Joanne. All she did was belt, but having heard her sing, warm up, and just mess around since rehearsal began, I knew Fredi had a warm, beautiful, and resonant head voice. I went to the piano for a bit and worked out a plan. I had to use part of the lyric of the song. It couldn't just be an "ooh" or an "aah," as that would feel disconnected from what everyone else was singing and sound meaningless. I took a couple of bits from the entire set of lyrics and spread them out over eight bars. From "Will I lose my dignity? / Will someone care? / Will I wake tomorrow from this nightmare?" I chose "Will I lose? Will someone care?"

Fredi joined me at the piano and we went through it a handful of times. At first I just wanted to find out if what I was hearing in my head was even the right idea, and then I wanted to let Fredi get it into her ear and her voice. It took a little longer than I had hoped, but the couple of times I glanced over at Arif, he seemed to be cool with whatever amount of time we needed, and he smiled a little bit when he heard it top to bottom. I was relieved that it didn't suck, given the amount of time we were taking up. The next thing was to have the band insert an extra eight bars near the end of the song, an easy task for them. We ran it down once and were ready to record, but Arif had another great idea, which was to have Kenny play the song on a twelve-string acoustic guitar (think "Hotel California" by The Eagles). So already we would be doing two things we couldn't replicate live every night at the theater. Recordings are so much more intimate, and those subtle choices by Arif were intended to be heard on a home stereo or headphones. The sonic results in the theater, especially with a rhythm section like ours, lent themselves better to broader brushstrokes.

The band tracked it without the vocals, and then the cast stepped into their booths. First, Gilles sang the solo as he had every night, beautifully and heart-wrenchingly, then he sang it joined by Toby and Byron, then by the next group, then the next, and so on, with the cast singing the extra verse. After it was all finished, Fredi stepped in and sang her new part over the last verse to the end of the song. She absolutely nailed it. One take. Gorgeous. Even though it was only eight bars, I was very proud of what I contributed to that song. A few nights later I tried to put it in the show. Of course it failed miserably and completely sucked the drama out of the end of the song. I *knew* it wasn't going to work, but I couldn't resist.

After all the large group numbers were done, we moved on to the small groups, duets, and solo numbers. First up, Anthony and Adam. Slaying it from the jump, from their "Tune Ups" all the way through the show to "What You Own." "Goodbye Love" contained what I referred to as the argument section between Mark and Roger, a long solo piano part (the bass entered about halfway in) that I had to play from memory. I had known that would be necessary prior to the recording. Turning all those pages at the session, even with a hired page turner, would have been too noisy with a half-open grand piano. Memorization, in all forms, is more a mental exercise than anything else. I knew how the song went; I could play it in my sleep. At least until the session. We got to a certain spot during "the argument," and because, I don't know, I was tired, I just lost focus for a split second. I made a mistake on two consecutive notes in the piano part. I had never done that before. But it was a great take by Adam and Anthony, so I couldn't stop. When that same music came around a second time, I made an executive decision: I made the identical mistake. If I screwed it up once, it was a mistake. If I screwed it up the same way again, it was music. Or as I told the band, "Once is a trend, twice is a part."

Late in the recording process, Fredi and Idina came in to record "Take Me or Leave Me." The band had already laid down the music bed, so it was just the two women singing. By this point, given that the show was difficult to sing in a big Broadway house, particularly eight times a week, and there was so much extra activity for everyone, some folks were a little beaten up vocally. This was true of Idina. Since our initial meeting at that first rehearsal, when we both brought along our club date clothes, I had always thought of her as my *much* younger, and certainly better-looking kid sister whom I was always looking out for. Not that she needed it. She was a great musician and she and Fredi were busy blowing the roof off the joint with "Take Me or Leave Me" every night, followed by the usual showstopping round of applause.

But Idina, by her own admission, was finding it hard to sustain night after night, simply because she'd never had to sing *that* high *that* often. I didn't help her much either, assigning her all the high female harmonies in the group numbers. She never called out. She just went in cycles. She'd be tremendous for a good stretch, then for a few days she sounded tired, then she'd recover. But the studio doesn't allow you to hide. It reveals any small flaw in a performance. The recording of "Take Me or Leave Me" reminded me of a famous John Lennon interview, where he talked about The Beatles's version of "Twist and Shout." At the end of the marathon *Please Please Me* session, having sung for almost twelve hours (with a cold), Lennon was down to his last vocal cord. He was singing way out of tune and obviously beyond tired, but he still produced an incredibly soulful, gritty, determined vocal. Like, I'm going to make this sound great and if I bleed on the microphone, all the better. Despite whatever flaws you could find in it (and you can), it is an undeniably electric rock and roll performance. The fact that it was captured live in a studio setting where everything was out there for all to hear made it a vocal that would stand the test of time.

The ladies did multiple takes of the song, and though Idina was getting more tired after each take, her own grittiness and tenacity had a slightly Lennon-esque "Twist and Shout" vibe. For the average listener, they wouldn't have heard that because, like always, she sang in tune. But when Arif and I listened to it closely, there was that raspy, I'm-on-the-edge performance—incredibly, indelibly soulful and record-worthy. And Fredi? She absolutely annihilated her vocal.

Soon enough, the vocals were done. Everyone had given great performances, a testament to a cast that was tired but fiercely dedicated. As busy and scattered as they were becoming outside the studio, inside those recording booths they were collected and focused. Jonathan would have been proud. I was. They all were. Sure, I think everyone wished they could have done this or that a little better—it's human nature. We wanted to be at our best always, and especially during those important weeks when we were laying it down for forever. I thought the cast and band made a great record. Personally, I was proud of a lot of stuff on it—"Will I?" foremost. In the not-so-proud column was obviously the "Goodbye Love" piano part, although I made the best of it. To the average listener it doesn't sound wrong, but those two notes *are* wrong, for all time.

I had been a little stuck since Jonathan passed, which was not my nature. On one hand I wanted the record to be as close as possible to the version of the music he'd heard the night before he died. But as I'd realized while compiling the vocal score, the show wasn't finished that night. It would continually reshape itself. Over time the cast had become more comfortable singing the songs, and subtle shifts in the music and vocals had begun to appear. The slightest musical and vocal changes would show up in the band and the cast. No one was making up riffs or anything like that just for the sake of trying something different. The cast and band had laid down and built up a solid musical foundation, and those slight deviances were just an outgrowth of the thing we had raised together. I knew a part of me was clinging to the past, for Jonathan or maybe for my own consolation. However, I also knew enough about rock, pop, R & B, and gospel to know that these styles are fluid. They're alive, which meant that *Rent*'s musical tapestry would be constantly, subtly maturing and unfolding. *Rent* was a living, breathing organism, continuously rearranging itself, but it would remain the same essential beautiful piece of art, no matter where it was in its musical evolution. Just as it was supposed to be.

The making of the cast album was joyous and satisfying, but it could never match the voltage and magic of our live performances. The finished studio product represented where we all were at a moment in time, a sonic photograph in the life of *Rent*.

1 year
4 seasons
12 months
52 weeks
365 days
1095 meals
8760 hours
525,600 minutes
31,536,000 seconds
            thoughts
            ideas   dreams
            breaths
            memories
            <u>moments that count</u>
how long is a moment?
what makes an event memorable?
<u>awareness</u>

Jonathan's math for "Seasons of Love."

STEVIE WONDER

WHILE THE CAST RECORDING WAS HAPPENING, there was some chatter going on about maybe having rock, R & B, and pop singers cover some of the *Rent* songs. Maybe as an entire CD, maybe as bonus tracks on the original cast album, or maybe just as songs that would show up on their own records. Of the many ideas out there, the ones I remember most were Cyndi Lauper, since she was a Brooklyn-Queens girl, but what would she sing? "Without You"? Yeah, that seemed like a good idea. How about Lou Reed singing "Santa Fe"? I'd definitely sign up for that. The other idea I liked was Paul Westerberg, the lead singer of The Replacements, singing "One Song Glory." The Replacements were a Minneapolis band that had been part of the emo/alt-rock style that had come out of the post-punk world of the 1980s. I thought of them as pre-grunge, especially live. Not a bad comp.

Amid that chatter we started hearing whispers that Stevie Wonder would be doing a version of "Seasons of Love." Those whispers turned into serious conversation after Arif confirmed it, the plan being that he would sing it with the cast. Not together of course. He'd sing with the track that we recorded for the cast album. I was dumbfounded by it. *Stevie Wonder.* The cast was thrilled, but bummed because they probably wouldn't meet him.

I had mentioned to Jonathan in our early conversations that Stevie was a big influence on my growth as a musician, not only because of his monstrous talents as a multi-instrumentalist but also his originality as a songwriter, arranger, and orchestrator. He heard so much, and not just his ridiculously multilayered rhythm section–based arrangements and production. There were stories about him working with other musicians and arrangers, singing them the iconic horn and string parts that became central to many of his songs. The fact that he heard seemingly everything inspired me to listen harder and transcribe what I heard better, all of which was essential to my musical growth. And then there was the voice. Stevie's was singular and incomparable. I dare anyone to listen to "You and I" or "Lately" and not be convinced that he was among the all-time great vocalists.

Jonathan hadn't shared my enthusiasm about Stevie Wonder. By his own admission he wasn't that deep into Motown or R & B. I was under the impression that he didn't gravitate to Stevie as an artist. Did he appreciate him as a songwriter? I'd asked. He did, but he said little beyond that and so we moved on.

Stevie was my guiding light as I came up through my teens and college years. I was a little late to the party, but after I fully devoured *Innervisions*, I went backward, as we musicians do, to learn more about this artist and his discography. I loved everything about his work: the piano and synth playing, the singing and songwriting, and that he was fluent in so many styles of music. He was pure prodigy. *Innervisions* contained everything an aspiring musician like me could want: superior songwriting, with jazz ("Too High"), Latin ("Don't You Worry 'Bout a Thing"), funk ("Higher Ground"), R & B ("Golden Lady"), and gospel ("He's Misstra Know-It-All"). The two ballads on that record, "Visions" and "All In Love Is Fair," were astonishing to me in their musical and poetic beauty. Then there was "Living for the City," which was by far the most theatrical song on the record. I must admit, when Jonathan and I talked about that song, I was surprised he didn't respond to its theatricality: the exposition in the verses, a scene in the middle, replete with underscoring, and a lyrical outcome in the last two verses that held up to the mirror everything that preceded it. Just like musical theater songwriting. The lyrics of the song were the narration of a life that, as a white person, I could witness and be empathetic to but never fully understand through my lived experience. So besides being a great song, it was socioculturally illuminating to a young man like me, and the coda of the song was haunting, musically and theatrically. After *Innervisions* I went back, starting with *Music of My Mind*, then *Talking Book* (featuring "You and I"), and continuing chronologically to *Fulfillingness' First Finale*. "Creepin'" from that record is my all-time favorite Stevie tune. It flew way under the pop radar. Then, of course, came the iconic *Songs in the Key of Life*. Like any Stevie devotee, I ate that record up like a pepperoni pizza. My cast vocal warmup included excerpts from "I Wish" and "Knocks Me Off My Feet." Even though Stevie Wonder didn't have any influence on the creation of *Rent*, his presence would be felt as long as I was around.

Prior to Stevie's recording "Seasons of Love," I got wind of some music biz stuff surrounding his participation, but the tiny bits Arif shared with me were way above my pay grade. I knew that negotiations were centered on a couple of major things: whether he could put the song out on his own record (he could but never did), and would he be the owner of the master tapes (he was).

As the cast recording was finishing up, Arif said to me in that peanut-buttery-smooth, Turkish American, bass-baritone voice of his, "Tim, you must be ready to come to the studio on a moment's notice. Stevie works on his own time clock and you must be on call twenty-four seven." It would just be Arif, Mike, Steve

Skinner, and me. Steve and Arif arranged and produced a funkier, extended version of the song and dropped the cast's vocals into it. The version they came up with was way more tilted toward modern R & B but still maintained the essence of Jonathan's song. It featured Anthony Jackson on bass and one of New York's finest session guitarists, Ira Siegel. The track was soulful, hip, and beautifully executed—highly appropriate for Stevie to sing over and right in his wheelhouse, though one could argue that everything was in his wheelhouse.

Arif, unfailingly classy and kind, said to me, "Tim, you need to be there. You're the musical director. You know everything about the music, and you know how it all goes." He was showing me respect for my place in the show, and I truly appreciated that, but, spoiler alert, Stevie Wonder didn't need me to be there. He'd be just fine. Still, Arif insisted, and at the end of that conversation, he said, and I'll never forget it as long as I live, "Tim, you can't miss this. There's going to be some once-in-a-lifetime shit that will happen, and you must be there to experience it." Up to then I hadn't known Arif to speak in such hyperbolic terms. Once-in-a-lifetime shit? He had my full attention.

While we waited for the call, the record still had to be mixed. Kenny had come in to do a daylong session's worth of overdubs, doubling parts using different models of guitars and amps to layer sounds on top of existing sounds. I laid down extra keyboard parts, Dan laid down extra guitar and organ parts, and Jeff laid down extra percussion. Record producers are like filmmakers: they want to have as much material as possible at their disposal so they have options to choose from when making final decisions on what to keep or discard in the final mix.

In the 1970s the audio company Eventide released its H910 Harmonizer onto the market and it was immediately recognized as a game changer in the recording industry. It could alter sounds and produce effects never before heard on a record. The 1994 model, the latest of many that Eventide had brought to market, contained a new feature called "vocal quantize" or, as it became commonly known, "pitch correction." You could run a vocal performance through it and the Harmonizer would "correct" the pitch to the closest note in the key in which the vocalist was singing. This was the beginning of what would become the ultra-popular auto-tune, which could alter the style of the singing itself (a memorable example being Cher's "Believe" in 1998). In the case of the original cast recording, I was amazed how the cast stepped up in the studio, after all they had been through. Despite their newly hectic lives, they persevered throughout the recording process, singing *in tune*, always. Except for one song. And to Arif and Mike's credit, that newfound pitch correction was applied with such a deft touch that it's virtually impossible to pick out which song it was. When I heard it, I couldn't believe what this revolutionary piece of technology could do. So, yes, there's a song that had to be electronically altered. I never told anyone which one it was.

The big decision about the mixing of the cast album ultimately came down to how the record should sound overall. This was a decision that had to involve the Larson family. Should it sound like a commercial rock record, like Sonic Youth's *Daydream Nation*, with the vocals tucked tightly into the music, or should it be more like a traditional theater record, where the vocals were further out in front of the orchestra, like on the *Company* cast album? There was a little back-and-forth between Arif, Kevin and Jeffrey, and the Larsons, but in the end it was an easy decision to make. Of course we would highlight the lyrics and put the vocals in front of the band, like more traditional theatrical recordings. The reasons for this were easy. First, the lyrics and their storytelling were complicated and it was important to give the listener the best chance to follow the stories. And second, this was Jonathan's posthumous masterwork and it needed to be understood. It was his songs, his melodies, and his lyrics. We had to honor that.

One morning early that summer, the phone rang, and it was Gloria Gabriel, Arif's album coordinator. Stevie would be at Right Track at 10:00 a.m., she told me. Nothing more to say. Although I'd been so busy, I had been waiting for that call with a last-day-of-school kind of anticipation. I didn't really know what to expect, other than what Arif had told me. All I knew was that it was going to be a great day.

I arrived at the studio early. We'd be in one of the smaller studios because all we needed was the control room and a space to record for one. I waited with Arif, Mike, and Steve, and right on the dot, at 10:00 a.m., Stevie came in with his guide, who doubled as his security dude. No entourage, just a professional musician showing up to do his magic. Yeah, it was Stevie Wonder, but on that day he was a singer and a chromatic harp player doing a recording session. The departure was, he was among the best in the world at both.

His associate left and there we were. It was an out-of-body experience that I remember like it was yesterday. He wore a dashiki, resplendent in the colors of the Ethiopian flag: red, green, yellow, and black, and the long braids he had at the time were beaded in the same colors as the dashiki. Arif introduced me by saying, "Stevie, this is Tim Weil, the musical director of the show. He knows every note and lyric in it." My inner response was, *Oh great, I'm the fucking lyric police for Stevie Wonder.*

He asked if someone could show him to the bathroom. "I have to get myself ready," he said and then added, "And I have to get rid of the percussion section," motioning to the beads. I walked him there, and when he returned he had tied up the braids with rubber bands and had put a big, baby-blue shower cap over his hair to dampen any unwanted sound even further.

MAKING RENT

Stevie had the lyrics printed in braille on a thick piece of paper and he took a seat at the recording console in the control room. Mike plugged a microphone directly into the console, routed it to its track, and Stevie told him, "While the first line of the song is playing, speak the next line into the mic, so I know what's coming. And when the next line comes in the music, speak the next line, and so on." This meant that while Stevie was singing a lyric (for example, "525,600 minutes"), what he was hearing in his headphones, besides his vocal and the track, was Mike speaking the following line ("525,000 moments so dear"). He was singing, creating, tracking the song, listening to the near future, and reading the lyric in braille *all at the same time.* Now that's what I call multitasking. He'd obviously listened to the song and knew the lyrics and melody, but he still had those backup systems in place.

He started by listening to the track Steve and Arif had created, with the cast's vocals on it. When he heard Gwen sing he remarked, "That girl sings pretty." I loved that. It was an extended version of the song, but something told me he had it figured out. Then he laid down his first take. He stuck to Jonathan's melody and rhythms, but sang it slightly different from the group vocals. Those tiny variations established him as the lead singer and the cast as the church choir.

After he completed the first pass, Arif asked me, "Tim, was that all right?" He meant it literally—did Stevie sing all the lyrics correctly? I thought, *Really? Do I have to?* Well, it was why I was there, so I guessed I had to. "Well, that lyric should be an 'a' instead of a 'the,'" I said. I'd never been more embarrassed in my life. I mean, it was my job, but did I have to say *that*? Stevie totally let me off the hook. "Okay," he said. "Gotta get all of those lyrics right, right?" He let me skate in a completely nonjudgmental, professional way. Stevie Wonder was a mensch.

The next take began, and he sang the first verse, again, as the lead singer, subtly different from the group. He sang the chorus and then began the second verse *an octave higher!* It came pouring out of him like water from a bucket. Nothing to it. Ethereal and breathtaking. At that point for me it started getting surreal. I was seeing this human being, this earthbound person, but the sound that he was channeling was from some faraway musical galaxy. That's when it all became crystal clear to me: what we are all trying to do as musicians living on this planet. It's to channel the music gods from a place none of us have seen, from a world we don't know exists, except we *know* that it holds some unspeakable truths that we can experience and share only through playing music. It's our lifelong mission to translate those truths into the best version of our musical selves. And Stevie Wonder is the shining example of that. The realization brought tears to my eyes and soon they were streaming down my face. They were tears of joy and amazement, and they wouldn't stop. I didn't mind. I couldn't believe I was there, experiencing the moment as a fanboy, a musician, and an artist. What was happening was just so beautiful. Stevie finished that incredible pass and went on, track after vocal track, each one different, and each one more transcendent than the one before, spinning musical gold. Each pass was a keeper by itself, but Arif wanted to record as much material as possible, so when it came time to mix he could do his best vocal composite. When Stevie had done about four complete passes, Arif asked if he wanted to take a break.

"No, I'm just gettin' warmed up!" Stevie declared. Indeed. He knew himself and his voice. He would continue to do another three or four passes. I was exhausted and he was just getting started.

An hour and a half into the session, the vocals were done. Stevie came back into the control room, and out it came at last: the chromatic harmonica or, in its shorthand, the chromatic harp. It's a harmonica that plays all twelve notes in an octave with a range of four octaves, as opposed to the regular harmonica, which plays only five notes over three octaves. Stevie set the standard when it came to playing chromatic harp in R & B, starting as a preteenager. His body of work on that instrument is legendary.

Stevie's chromatic harps were custom-made for him. The smallest details of each tailored to his needs: its size and weight, the diameter of the holes he blew through, the way it fit in his hands, and the overall feeling that the instrument was an extension of him. The one he brought with him that day was in a sterling silver case with gold trim and had "Wonder Harp XVII" etched on it. When he opened the case, it was like the scene in *Pulp Fiction* where Samuel L. Jackson opens the briefcase at the diner and it releases blinding golden rays of light. That's what I felt when Stevie opened it. And of course I heard the chorus of angels singing. It was all that. An event unto itself. Stevie took the harp out and didn't even need to warm up because he'd been breathing plenty for close to two hours. After Arif walked him back into the studio, got him set up, and the track started playing, off I went again, onto the Stevie Wonder Joy Ride of Otherworldly Artistry.

The intro to the song began and Stevie started playing beautiful fills, simple in their beauty, never repetitive or clichéd, and always inspired. Then the vocals came in (with one of Stevie's leads along with the cast) and his harp flirted with them, darted in and out of them, and complemented them. He connected them to each other when necessary, shorter and longer phrases, each musically complete on its own terms. Not a speck of waste. In that extended version of the song, they gave a full verse to Stevie for a harp solo. He probably played four or five passes, each one as good as or better than what had come before. I thought, *Which vocal, which harp track would you choose?* Truly an embarrassment of musical riches with every note, every breath, every twist and turn of phrase. He channeled his harp playing just as he had channeled his vocals. That sound was so distinctly *his*, and there

I went again, the tears streaming down my face. I thought back to when I was younger, and all of his harp playing: "Fingertips, Part 2," "For Once in My Life," "I Was Made to Love Her," "If It's Magic," Chaka Kahn's "I Feel for You," and the incredible solo on the outro of "Isn't She Lovely." Seven choruses! Even "That's What Friends Are For," a song about the AIDS crisis from long before *Rent*. Prescient.

After another hour or so, he had tracked more than anyone could ask for. All of it virtuosic, creative, inspirational, and awe-inspiring. He felt and understood the entirety of that song. Its message, its beating heart, Jonathan's beating heart, and he poured himself into it completely. His final lyrics, "Jonathan wrote about it. / We're singin' about it. / He wrote about it. / And we're singin' about it. Whoa . . . ," and then the *ridiculous* harp phrases he laid down over the last chorus, swerving among the cast vocals to the end of the song. He is everything musicians strive to become: innovative and truthful, playing with purity and freedom. And then, just like that, he packed up Wonder Harp XVII, took off his shower cap, said his goodbyes, and his escort took him away. Once-in-a-lifetime shit indeed.

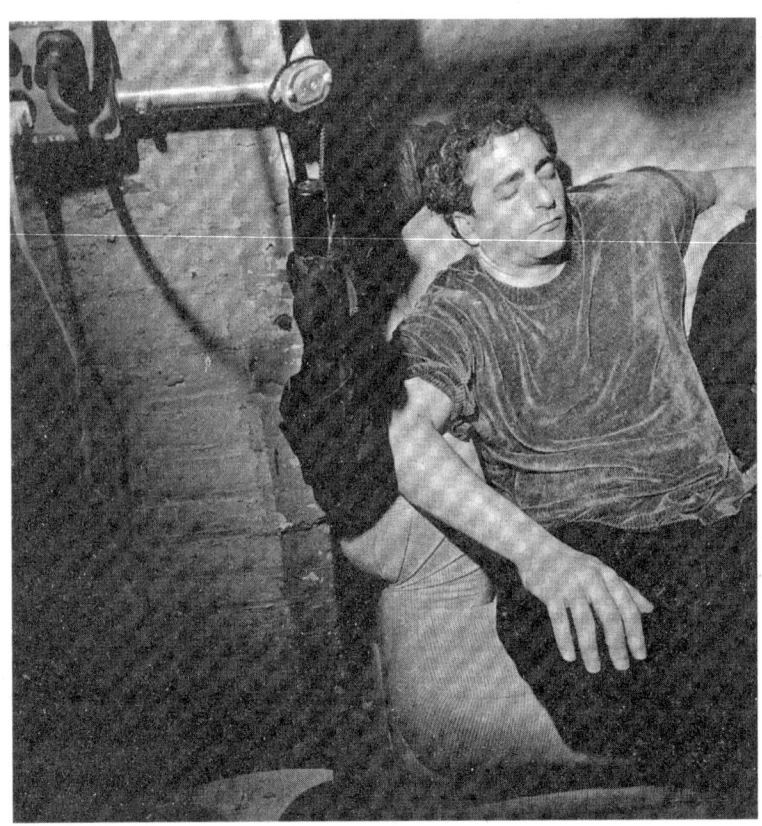
Me, doing my finest work, ten minutes before curtain, 1996.

RUNNING
1996–2015

AFTER OUR OPENING, while we worked on the original cast recording and did all our media over the ensuing weeks, we were playing to standing-room-only houses. Everything that was happening on a nightly basis felt very much like the Workshop to me, except with more than six times the audience attending every show. The Nederlander had a capacity of just over twelve hundred, plus standing room in the back of the orchestra section. The cast members all handled their new rock star status with ease. They had tasted it downtown, which was kind of rock star 101, but as we got into our Broadway run, some stuff got downright dopey. One night Steph came out at 7:55, tuned her basses, and then warmed up quietly, rehearsing her "Santa Fe" bass part because it was by far the most unnatural and difficult song for the bassist to play in the show. She warmed up with it, and the audience whooped and applauded! I mean, that's a little beyond, right? Clapping for the bass player's warmup? Not since The Who's "My Generation." For a minute there, Steph was John Entwistle.

As we sailed through the spring months, we were aware that award season was coming up. Because we had been both off and on Broadway in the 1996 season, we were eligible for both the Obie (off Broadway) and the Tony (Broadway) awards. On May 20 the show won three Obie awards: Outstanding Book, Music, and Lyrics; Outstanding Direction; and the one I was happiest about, Outstanding Ensemble Performance. Yes, Jonathan's work was life-changing and Michael's direction was superior, but I just loved that the awards committee saw the whole of us and recognized the community. It was becoming clear by that time that Adam, Daphne, Anthony, Taye, Idina, Jesse, Wilson, and Fredi would all get a little more attention by the entertainment press and the public. Truth was, as much as we all considered ourselves to be of one quilt, that wasn't the case for those who viewed the show as any other show would have been seen. There were principal performers who stood out from the full group and the less-highlighted ensemble roles in the show. Jonathan had done his best to feature everyone who was onstage, and Michael carried his vision through, which was enormously successful, but in the end everyone got compartmentalized by both the people who were giving out trophies and the audiences. That's show business. Awards are as much about marketing and publicity for the plays as they are recognition of the piece. In my mind everyone should have received every award, but that Obie for Outstanding Ensemble Performance was the next best thing.

The week prior to the Obie trophies, the Tony nominations came out. So much had happened in the past three months and here was the next event. *Rent* was nominated for ten Tony awards: Best Musical, Best Score, Best Book, Best Direction, Best Lighting Design (awesome for Blake, who came out of the downtown club scene), Best Choreography (great for Marlies, who also was not from the mainstream Broadway community), and a small pile of acting nominations for Idina, Daphne, Wilson, and Adam. We won four of those awards. Two for Jonathan (Best Book and Best Score), Best Supporting Actor for Wilson, and Best Musical

MAKING RENT

for our producers, which much to my delight, besides Kevin and Jeffrey, included the New York Theatre Workshop. Jonathan's sister, Julie, gave the acceptance speech. I didn't know her well at the time, but she spoke beautifully on behalf of Jonathan and his family, whom we had met and I was getting to know better.

In our first few months at the Nederlander, the one area we couldn't get on top of was the sound. We knew there were sound problems while we were running downtown, but because of the intimacy of that 199-seat theater we got by. When we moved uptown, those problems got worse because we were playing in a much more cavernous space. At intermission, after the act one bombardment of sound and the disappointing lack of lyrical clarity, many people in the audience either complained to the front-of-house sound engineer, simply walked out, or both—many asking for refunds. After the show ended, there were more complaints, and subsequently many letters were sent to the producers echoing the same sound issues and demands. Alongside our sound designer, Kurt Fischer, we attacked the issue as best we could. In this particular case, I was part of the problem, not the solution.

Kurt had monitors all over the stage. Monitors are small speakers, varying in size, that are placed in strategic spots onstage for the actors to hear the band. Kurt had put them everywhere: across the front, on the sides, up above the Life Support platform, and in Mimi's "loft," an elevated area upstage center. My hope was that we could put as much sound as anyone wanted in any of those monitors. All the actors wanted to hear themselves first, then certain instruments second. Each actor had different wants and needs, and I was trying to accommodate all of them, saying yes to everything. Kurt wanted to placate me as well, but he knew that fulfilling my requests was an impossible task. There were too many vocals going through too many open microphones, especially during the larger group numbers, and the amplifiers on the bandstand were making too much noise of their own, resulting in a giant, echoey mess. The result of all those swirling echoes onstage was sonic mayhem in the house, and *that's* what made the lyrics unintelligible to so many audience members. After Kurt schooled me in those acoustical realities, he took the actors' vocals out of the monitors and the problems quickly dissipated. He also asked that the band try to play a little quieter onstage, which would help the audience understand the show better, and he promised that the energy and the decibel levels wouldn't suffer, that in fact it would give the front-of-house mixer more control of the musical output.

After we made those changes, the complaints and letters became less frequent. They never fully went away, but we decided as a group—producers included—that part of what made *Rent* was its rock concert–like quality wrapped in a Broadway show. It was what Jonathan and all of us wanted, and it was important that we stuck to that identity. Our show ran at a higher decibel level than anything that had preceded it. I proclaimed, self-righteously, that the show wasn't for the faint of heart, and if you can't take it, go see *Annie*. The show continued to improve sonically, now that we all were more attentive to the realities of our spacious Broadway theater.

Even with the sound issues finally mostly solved, some audience members still left during act one or at intermission. As was the case in our downtown run, people would leave when they saw men kissing men or women kissing women, and there was still some discomfort around HIV/AIDS and the AIDS activism that was front and center, especially in "La Vie Boheme." There were others, of course, who had different reasons not to return for act two. During the intermission of a Saturday matinee in the summer of 1996, a friend of mine overheard two ladies talking about the show (theater people refer to them affectionately as "matinee ladies"). One said to the other, "Let's see: they're young, they're on drugs, and they can't pay their rent. Why are we here?"

The summer was a welcome respite for a lot of us. I settled into my routine: answer the phone, do the gig, continue writing the score, and be with Randy whenever I could. As Randy and I were getting closer, I was, in my private moments, constantly thinking back twelve months earlier. No apartment, just a rented room, no money at all, and not much work to speak of (certainly none of it steady), betting my hopes on weekly meetups with Jonathan, auditioning actors at Bernie's office. I marveled at how much had changed. I marveled at *change*. I was finally beginning to appreciate each day with a little more gratitude. I wasn't quite up to the "no day but today" ethos of the show, but I was taking baby steps in my appreciation for the life I was living. I felt more present.

During the summer a couple of significant things happened. In July Idina called out of the show, our first cast absence since rehearsals had begun in December 1995. It was a little devastating but inevitable. Once that dam had broken, and with scheduled vacations beginning to happen, we got used to the new normal. Fortunately, no one left the cast permanently until the spring of 1997, but once it started, it went quickly. First Idina, then, one after another, Daphne, Jesse, Gilles, and Taye, and on it went. By the end of 1997 we had lost nine of the originals and we would lose more as we moved into the next year. Opportunities were out there for these incredible young talents, and of course they had to chase them down. Before replacing those departing cast members, however, Bernie and his growing company were consumed with the casting of the first national tour of *Rent*, which was to begin rehearsals in late September 1996 and open in Boston in late November.

While we were casting that first national tour, the show had become popular in ways that I'd never seen or imagined. Since I hadn't been around for *A Chorus Line*, *The Phantom of the Opera*, or *Les Misérables*, I had never understood how insanely popular a Broadway show could get or how Broadway fandom could manifest. To attract younger theatergoers who couldn't afford the price of a Broadway ticket, Kevin and Jeffrey had set up a system in which the first two rows of the theater would go on sale for twenty dollars a seat, two hours before curtain, at 6:00 p.m. on weekdays and noon on matinee days. It was quite the marketing and publicity strategy and exactly what Jonathan would have wanted. *Rent* became a portal through which the MTV generation could get access to, and be turned on by, a Broadway musical. The discount ticket policy was instigated when we began previews in April and quickly got to a point where, when the band emerged from the theater on a Wednesday night, there would already be a long line of young people with sleeping bags, food, water, and dope waiting for the Thursday drawing. Those first two rows would have sold out in a New York minute, but our producers were committed to their idea of making musical theater accessible for the less-well-off but no-less-eager audiences.

Before long the weekends started to reveal a larger problem. Because we had two shows on Saturday and two on Sunday, Thursday night would be the beginning of the formation of three lines, all winding around the block. Line one was for the Friday-night show, line two was for the Saturday matinee, and line three was for the Saturday-night show. Sometime early on Saturday, the two lines for the Sunday performances would begin to form. All of that organized chaos for *thirty-four seats*. I don't know why the city allowed it and I'm sure that the phenomenon came as a complete surprise to them, but they had no policy in place to stop it. The whole crowded experiment went surprisingly smoothly for a little while, but by the early summer, some weird yet predictable things started to happen.

Because the neighborhood around our theater was still underdeveloped, there were drug addicts, homeless people, and a mentally ill population that started harassing our sidewalk enthusiasts, many of whom had only heard about the show from their friends. Since the recording wasn't out yet, they didn't know the show other than from word of mouth by previous audience members or bootleg recordings they had copped from the dedicated fans who came to be known as Rentheads. At a certain point, our loyal sleepover following needed real security. Fortunately the NYPD came to the rescue and soon uniformed cops would patrol the area whenever the lines started to get long, even remaining there through the night and into the early morning.

As the spring and summer wore on, the whole, endless living-in-line thing started to take on a *Lord of the Flies* quality. It became a culture within a culture. People would pay for a place in the line, or make offers of food, drink, and drugs for a spot. It had its own hierarchy and its own internal rules and regulations. The stuff I heard was happening out there was nihilistic. That continued through the summer, fall, and even winter, but finally in the late spring of 1997, Kevin and Jeffrey came up with a new and better plan, so that exercise finally came to an end. People could arrive any time after the box office opened at 10:00 a.m. and put their name in the "hat" for that night's eight-o'clock show. That same pattern was repeated (time-adjusted of course) for our crazy weekend schedule. The reasoning was fair and simple: in the old setup, normal nine-to-five workers could never get access to those lottery tickets. The new scheduling apparatus gave them a fairer shake at the twenty-dollar prize. I'm sure the NYPD was happy that the system had changed, but they had done their duty and served our loyal Rentheads, truly protecting them for about ten months. All of us in the band couldn't believe that over the previous year, no one got hurt, stabbed, or killed. We were sure there was intimidation but, thankfully, no blood. It was a fantastic attempt at utopian socialism.

TIM WEIL

The original cast album came out in late August 1996. It sold incredibly well, especially by theater standards. We achieved gold record status (500,000 units sold) quickly, and not long after, it went platinum (1,000,000 units sold) and sales continued on from there. We even reached double platinum status (2,000,000) just one year after its release. The cast album finally got the material out to the public, so people could hear the show as many times as they wanted before they saw it while following along with the libretto, neatly packaged in the two-CD set. It was a packaging approach reminiscent of that for opera recordings, which similarly enabled opera lovers to study a libretto at home before attending the opera. It seemed to me that, with people now taking a similar approach to our show, our rock opera bona fides were cemented.

The newly released CD also meant that people who were auditioning for the show could have a thorough listen to the songs they were going to have to learn. I had finally finished writing out the vocal score after the album was mixed and sent it to the copyist, so we were able to give out written material for the people who would be auditioning. Prior to that, Bernie's office would have to coordinate with our management to arrange for the people who got called back to come to the theater, stand in the back, and watch the show. We had no other means by which they could digest the music, so when the album and sheet music became available, the songs quickly made their way out to the public. Just in time for the next level of craziness.

In the summer of 1996 Kevin and Jeffrey's strategy of striking while the iron was hot led to the first of our many touring companies of *Rent*. The first national tour was referred to as the Angel Company. Touring productions would often be named alphabetically by character, so our first American company was Angel, the second was Benny, and the third, which toured Canada, was Collins.

MAKING RENT

Since the Telsey office on West Twenty-Eighth Street was too small to handle their massive audition traffic now that *Rent* had blown up, they had to hold their auditions offsite. Union auditions were held at Chelsea Studios, just a couple of blocks from their office, and the open calls (which means what it sounds like—open to anyone who wanted to audition, just like in the 1994 version) were held at Musical Theater Works, down in the East Village on Lafayette Street, across from the Public Theater. When I went down there, I remember thinking, *This place looks familiar.* Back in the 1980s I had accompanied ballet and modern dance classes when the place was called DancerSchool, owned and operated by the choreographer Dennis Wayne. I learned a lot doing that, and for a while it was as steady a gig as I had. Now, there I was again, almost fifteen years later and under completely different circumstances.

Bernie, Will, David, and now Heidi Marshall, their newly hired casting associate, had prescreen auditions in four separate rooms, and they went for hours at a time. There were a few reasons why that was necessary, but the biggest one was that since it was an open call, there were tons of people standing outside waiting to audition. The line stretched out the door and down Lafayette to East Fourth, where it took a right turn toward Broadway, another right onto Broadway, went up another four blocks to Eighth Street, made another right back toward Lafayette, then a right turn until it got back down to the entrance of the building. Doing that geography, you had to stand, move, stand, and shuffle ten city blocks to get in to audition with your sixteen-bar cut of music. Not only were the people wrapped all around that ten-block area, but they were wrapping around it a *second* time. That's how crowded it was. Bernie told me that at any point every day of auditions, there could be as many as four thousand people waiting in line. *Four thousand!* The good thing was that it was early summer, so at least they weren't out there in the cold for hours.

Also, Bernie had brought down several of the interns who were working at MCC to act as monitors for the crowd. They were stationed at various points of the audition route and handed out bottled water and pizza to those who came empty-handed. How were they to know that when they arrived, instead of just walking into the building, they had to start somewhere in that urban rectangle to begin their long expedition to the audition room?

Those open calls were a great decision by Bernie and Will. Our original cast from the 1994 production had a small handful of people with their Equity cards, and our 1995–96 group had a number of cast members who had to join Actors' Equity as well when we moved from NYTW to the Nederlander. Bernie had been very successful finding nonunion actors, so he knew there was gold out there in the open-casting world, and now he and his crew knew exactly where to find them. But, by the time the summer of 1996 came around, the people were coming to us. All of Bernie's initial casting work informed what our future companies would look, feel, and sound like. There was a template in place for who would populate the first touring company, and we could make it tighter, sleeker, and more efficient. Having more of the onstage cast covering more roles, with offstage covers playing a wider variety of roles, is standard and necessary for touring productions, whose expenses, mostly due to travel and schedule, are higher. We eventually cast the Angel Company, with a few Equity actors and a lot of non-Equity actors. It would be a great opportunity for all of them, very much in the mold of the Broadway company. For some of them it was their first show, for some of them their first tour, and for all of them their first Tony-winning hit show that would reach more people than would ever see it on Broadway because the major touring houses around the country tended to be quite a bit larger. Another huge benefit was they would make good, steady money on the road, so for many of those young performers it would mean they could really sock away some cash early in their professional life if they chose. It could provide a much-needed cushion for them when they returned to New York or wherever they lived.

My job, when I wasn't musical director for the Broadway company, was music supervisor, which meant I had to organize everything music-related to the touring productions, first and foremost hiring musical directors, touring bands, and where necessary, local musicians. Every major city had its own rules and regulations about the use of local players. The American Federation of Musicians, the musicians' union, existed on both the local and national levels. The local unions were responsible for their own rules. Since we weren't regarded as a self-contained band in certain cities with stronger unions, we often had to go through a local music contractor. The places where we absolutely had to hire locally were Boston, Chicago, and San Francisco, and sometimes Los Angeles, depending on which theater we were playing. Also, we had to respect the minimum number of musicians required, which varied from theater to theater. In San Francisco, for instance, we played the Golden Gate Theatre, which required a minimum of ten musicians. So with our musical director still allowed to play from the conductor's chair, we had to hire nine others, even though we only needed four. For those weeks, we had to put our touring band on hiatus. I asked the local contractors if we could hire those extra people and have them learn the books, so we would have subs already in place when we needed them. They were all incredibly accommodating, not knowing me from Adam, and allowed me to hold auditions. They weren't required to do that, but because our show needed a certain kind of player and this grunge rock band concept was new to contemporary theater, they were as cooperative as I could've hoped. The local Boston, Chicago, and San Francisco bands were all great. It was nice to meet and make friends with musicians from all over the country, a perk that I hadn't anticipated when we embarked on that next phase of the show.

Everything didn't go as we'd planned or hoped for with our initial touring company. First, we had to fire the young man who played Roger. As lovely a guy as he was and as beloved as he was by the company, he couldn't sing the notes required of him eight shows per week. Sadly, not even for two or three shows. We knew when we cast him that he'd need help (which he got), but he never got over the vocal hump of it, and Michael, Kevin, Jeffrey, and I decided, after much discussion, that we couldn't set the precedent this early in *Rent*'s touring life of changing keys or melodies. I felt I'd be letting Jonathan down a little too early. I remember thinking that if it had been a year or so later then, yeah, we'd adjust. It was bad timing for us and this young man. Another actor had some personal problems offstage that had to get straightened out, so we had to let that person go as well. It was a couple of huge blows to a cast that they didn't deserve, and Michael and I got a lot of heat for it. But we did what we felt was best in the big picture for the show. An even bigger blow to this company would come a few years later, in 2002, when Carrie Hamilton (Carol Burnett's daughter), who was a fantastic Maureen for the show's first tour, developed lung cancer and passed away. It was shortly after she left the show, and even though most of the company had moved on by then, all of them remained friends and Carrie had been a galvanizing force in the legacy of that group. Her death was a kick in the teeth for a company who took on more water than they ever expected or deserved. Michael and I learned that the touring lives of the *Rent* companies that followed would all experience varying degrees of success and challenges.

In 1997 we hatched the second national tour, cast first in New York but mostly cast out of Los Angeles. They debuted with a short run at the La Jolla Playhouse in San Diego, where Michael was still the artistic director, followed by an opening at the famed Ahmanson Theatre in Los Angeles, where they played to sold-out houses for sixteen weeks, an amazing way to launch that production. As with the first tour, Bernie and company auditioned thousands of people. Los Angeles was brimming with actors who wanted to be in TV and film, but deep in their hearts many of them were real musical theater geeks, and with auditions in their city they came out in droves. The result was that we did many fourteen-hour audition days. And because Bernie, Heidi, Michael and I enjoyed each other's company so much, after each day of auditions we often continued our conversation over drinks and Mexican food. As hard as Michael and I were working, I always reminded myself that Bernie and Heidi were working twice as hard. Those auditions were indeed a grind, but fun. Honestly, I eagerly anticipated the opportunities and possibilities that each day would bring, and in the end we had another great cast, including Neil Patrick Harris, who would play Mark, and an incredible band.

On and on it went. In 1997 we launched the Canadian company in Toronto, and in 1998 the London cast, who opened their tour by playing the Shaftesbury Theatre in London's West End, with Anthony, Adam, Jesse, and Wilson all agreeing to go over with Michael and me to be a part of that company. They stayed for a year; then our UK cast rode it out. Also in 1998, Martha Banta, associate choreographer Schele Williams, and I were sent to Tokyo to mount a production with an all-Japanese company, complete with a Japanese translation (our show was difficult to translate with all the Americanisms, colloquialisms, curse words and rhyming schemes) and projected English supertitles. It was the most fantastic time I had ever experienced outside the United States, and the worst. Once again, joy and tragedy, happiness and utter shock returned.

Schele was a bit of a jock with a mad theater skillset. She had been the dance captain on our first national tour, and Marlies, quickly and smartly, tagged her to be her associate choreographer for the tours she was unable to do. Schele and I were both big baseball fans, and we agreed beforehand to bring our gloves to Japan so we could play catch on rehearsal breaks. It was in the middle of one of those games of catch that my oldest brother called.

"Hey, it's Joe. Are you sitting down?"

"Well, I can't really. I'm playing catch behind a loading dock in a parking lot here in Tokyo."

Joe didn't care about any of those minor details. "Mom's sick," he said. "She's got lung cancer."

My heart (and glove) dropped to the concrete.

"Remember when she got radiation for her lumpectomy last year?" Joe continued. "Well, apparently there was some leakage and the cancer is on a place on her lung where they can't get to it. The doctors are already talking about her quality of life." I was stunned. This was like some 1970s medical drama where the husband says, "What's the prognosis, doctor? How long does she have?" The beautiful, clear sunny day in Tokyo instantly felt thick and hazy.

Then, just like that, our break was over and it was time to get back to work. Had we been doing an English version of the show, it would have been easier for me to jump back into rehearsal, focus on the work, and compartmentalize the bad news I'd just received from Minnesota. Since we were doing the show in Japanese I was able to check out for periods of time and let my mind wander and worry. The Japanese musical director spoke a little English and we had interpreters around, so I could catch enough of what was happening to stay loosely connected to the rehearsal and choose the degree to which I concentrated on the work.

Truth is, as distraught as I was from my brother's call, I was still having a blast. I felt a little guilty about my enjoyment of all things Japanese (ramen and Starbucks) while my folks were dealing with my mom's terrible prognosis, but not *that* guilty. It was my first time in Japan, a place I'd always wanted to visit (I had a lot of Japanese friends from my years at the conservatory), and I was having a ton of fun doing my first production of the show with Martha, who by then was firmly ensconced as the associate director. She was a great director and was the one who had originally called me to be the audition pianist at the Workshop, the person I'd known longest in my *Rent* tenure. During our time away from rehearsal I told her about my mom, and I leaned into Schele and her for emotional support. They responded to my bad news from home in their kind, always-caring ways.

In a happy turn of events, Jonathan's father, Al, came over for the opening. He and I had grown close since the summer of 1996, having instantly liked each other, and we talked on the phone often. When we met in the cities where the tours were playing, we'd watch the show and always stay out late, partying to varying degrees with the cast, band, and management.

Our relationship would never fill the void that Jonathan's death left for him, but our companionship made me feel like a second son and he a second father. I called Al "Pop," and he called me "Sonny" or the occasional "Timmy," just like he had called Jonathan "Jonny." Pop was in his seventies by then, but he was still feisty. An old-school bar beast, Pop would drink, hang, and proudly wear the mantle of Jonathan's father, and by extension *Rent*'s godfather, and he was eager to talk to anyone who wanted to know about Jonathan and his hit musical, all of which made him very happy. Pop deserved all the happiness he could squeeze out of a performance and the night at a bar afterward. It was his therapy. We hung out in London with Nan and their extended family, where he also met and spent time with my folks, whom I had brought over for that opening, so it was great to be with him again in Tokyo. I looked after Pop as any son would look after an aging father, but he would never give himself over to that dynamic, so I just stayed close, watchful, and attentive when we were together. When I shared what had happened with my mom earlier that week, he was incredibly empathetic.

Although my mother's prognosis was dire, during those

weeks in Tokyo, my focus was on presenting Jonathan's work in the best way I could, especially in musical theater–crazed Japan, whose audiences were seeing *Rent* for the first time. Japanese people loved the American musical art form. I had no idea why. I knew their culture loved jazz—there's a long history of rare Japanese-made albums that were gold in America, records that were an important part of any serious jazz aficionado's collection—but the musical theater obsession came as a complete surprise to me.

While my brother's phone call was the worst I had ever received, the sting of it was offset by a couple of memorable things around my first Japanese experience with the show. One came on the first day of rehearsal when our Japanese musical director told me in his brave but halting English that his parents owned a New York–style delicatessen nearby. Because of that, every day he had to leave rehearsal from 11:30 a.m. to 2:00 p.m. to help them make and serve New York–style sandwiches, slabs of bread piled high with deli meat just like their American counterparts. He said that his parents' deli was the most famous deli in Tokyo. I couldn't believe there was much competition for that title, but my real concern was that he had a pianist to cover for him while he was working with his family six days a week (he did). One day I went over to the deli on our lunch break and found out he wasn't kidding about its popularity. The line to get a sandwich wrapped around the block. It was like the *Rent* open call on Lafayette Street, only it wasn't for a role in the show; it was for a pastrami on rye.

When we got to the point of doing run-throughs, we'd either gather for cast notes the following day or at the end of that day's rehearsal, time permitting. After our final dress rehearsal our crew still had work to do in the theater, so Martha, Schele, and I took our note session to the theater lobby. Once there we saw a massive number of stunning bouquets of flowers that had been delivered, presumably as opening-night gifts for all the performers. Along with the flowers, there were thirty or so large, beautifully painted cans filled about three-quarters of the way up with water, presumably for the flowers, equally spaced along the half-moon shape of the lobby wall. The flowers were gorgeous, but I couldn't figure out why they weren't in the water. Once our wonderful, groovy Japanese cast slowly ambled out for notes, they sat down next to the cans. Most of the cast members were young entertainment industry celebrities, so I assumed their people would come to match the correct bouquet to the correct can and in turn to the correct actor. But no sooner had they sat down than almost every one of them lit up a cigarette, and within minutes all of them were chain-smoking and discarding their cigarettes into their water cans. Martha, Schele, and I looked sideways at each other, like, *Is this really happening?* As we disseminated notes, cigarette smoke was wafting through the cramped enclosure like the Southern California coast's marine layer. I got out of that note session smelling like I had been living inside a hookah. After we were done and everyone left the theater Martha, Schele, and I couldn't hold it in any longer. We stood there talking about what had just transpired, and we lost it. I loved that group, that band, and that production. Sure enough, by the next night all the bouquets had indeed been set in those same cans—hopefully after their cleaning—and delivered to the actors' dressing rooms.

Shortly after we opened, I flew back to New York, then headed straight on to Minneapolis to see my folks. I didn't stop working for long though, as the touring companies kept coming. In 1998 we also did tours in Australia and Germany (the latter another one for Martha and me; we never did an English-speaking version of the show together); then in 1999, Mexico City and Barcelona; and in 2000, Milan. There were so many productions in the first handful of years that if we kept naming them alphabetically, we might have easily gotten to the Maureen Company and maybe as far as the Squeegee Man Company.

So much had happened since Jonathan died in early 1996, with the seemingly endless parade of events overlapping. Between the move uptown, the awards, the show's runaway commercial success, and the tours in and out of North America (*Rent* was already well on its way to being performed in over fifty countries around the world, but no, I didn't do anywhere near all of them), it fell upon Jonathan's family and friends to become the surrogates who did the press, interviews, and acceptance speeches for the many awards and honors Jonathan and *Rent* received, as well as traveling to as many countries as possible for the different international openings. The lion's share of that responsibility fell on Al, Nan, and Julie, and they would ask Jonathan's friends Jonathan Burkhart, Victoria Leacock, Todd Robinson, Eddie Robinson, Barry Singer, and Jonathan's closest friend from childhood, Matt O'Grady, to step in whenever and wherever they could. Al, Nan, and Julie embraced so many of the events and circumstances that flew at them like a tornado, rather than shying away from it all amid the pain of their grief. They saw many of those occasions that they had to show up for as opportunities to help others. As I would come to learn early on, the Larsons were driven by their deep commitment to humanity. Whether it was their support for research to help people and families dealing with Marfan syndrome or setting up a foundation to give financial awards to artists who needed a helping hand, just as Jonathan had received on his way up, they did what they felt needed to be done, no matter the circumstances.

From early April 1996, when Al received a letter from the National Marfan Foundation (NMF, today the Marfan Foundation) to August of 1999, the Larsons had been working closely with the foundation and the New York State Department of Health, trying to get more clarity about the cause of Jonathan's death. On August 12, 1999, Al appeared on *Good Morning America* and said the

Larsons' had come to believe that "Jonathan had died due to Marfan syndrome or a closely related connective tissue disorder" and announced they would be making a significant donation to the foundation in Jonathan's name. In December of 1999 Jonathan's cause of death was officially changed from an aortic aneurysm to "an aortic dissection, believed to have been caused by Marfan syndrome." That change appeared in Jonathan's bio in the *Playbill* for *Rent* and other publications from that point on.

The watershed moment occurred in July of 1996, when ABC's weekly news program, *Primetime Live* told Jonathan's story, and the public saw for the first time what the Larsons and the foundation had already seen: the X-ray showing the ten-inch tear in Jonathan's aorta that went overlooked by the hospital. That program re-aired on Christmas Day later that year.

Between the enormous popularity of *Rent,* and bolstered by the *Primetime Live* piece, stories of Jonathan and his untimely death appeared everywhere, from television shows and magazines to the rapidly exploding internet. This proved to be a real turning point in Marfan awareness. Parents and young people alike saw themselves in pictures of Jonathan. They recognized their own unique physical features that are typical of people with Marfan syndrome: unusual height, disproportionately long arms and legs, large hands and long fingers, and, in some cases, hyperextensible elbows, hips, and knees. Sure enough, many successful diagnoses followed, leading to many lives being saved. Just as Magic Johnson's HIV diagnosis brought an understanding of HIV/AIDS into popular culture in ways only an iconic sports luminary could, Jonathan's Marfan diagnosis had a similar effect in the public square and medical circles.

Today there are over two hundred thousand people in the United States with Marfan syndrome, along with other genetic disorders having to do with the aorta and other vascular conditions. The Marfan Foundation continues to thrive, and although no one in the Larson family would say it, they were a big part of the growth in the recognition, diagnosis and treatment of the disease in the late 1990s and over the next decades. As Al said to me early in our relationship, "We want to make sure that what happened to Jonny never happens to anyone again."

Also in the wake of Jonathan's death, the Larsons also set up the Jonathan Larson Performing Arts Foundation, an endowment for theater artists—composers, librettists, and lyricists—that distributes grants to artists for their originality, creativity, craft, and skill. There are no restrictions on what an artist can submit. While I was on the selection committee its first few years, I read and listened to everything from a clarinet, banjo, bass and drum quartet to a fully fleshed out musical and everything in between. If an artist could imagine it and present it, the panel would listen to it. Since Jonathan's music was contemporary, I tended to lean into that aesthetic during those early years, but we didn't by any means discard the more traditional musical theater submissions. Unlike the Richard Rodgers Award that Jonathan had won, there were no conditions or requirements on how the award money was spent or allocated. Whatever the grant winners thought would move their work forward: from buying pencils, music software, or recording gear to producing a reading or workshop, it didn't matter.

Because Jonathan's career had occasionally been bolstered by the grants, commissions, and awards he won, the foundation was a natural outgrowth of his career legacy. Although all of Jonathan's family and friends loved and supported the foundation, it was especially Nan whom it appealed to, as Julie told me. After 2008 the Jonathan Larson Performing Arts Foundation was folded into the American Theatre Wing (which presents the Tony Awards, along with a wide array of other theater and outreach programs), where it became the Jonathan Larson Grant. Past winners of the grant who have become well known in musical theater circles include Matthew Sklar (*Elf, The Prom*), Shaina Taub (*Suffs, The Devil Wears Prada*), Benj Pasek and Justin Paul (*Dear Evan Hansen*), Laurence O'Keefe (*Legally Blonde*), Joe Iconis (*Be More Chill*), Tom Kitt and Brian Yorkey (*Next to Normal*), Michael R. Jackson (*A Strange Loop*), and Steven Lutvak (*A Gentleman's Guide to Love and Murder*). Happily, it will operate in perpetuity under the Wing's stewardship. Another way the Larsons continued to pay it forward is the scholarship that Adelphi University, Jonathan's alma mater, awards every year in his name. Initially a bequest from the Larson Family Trust initiated in 2011, it finally came to fruition in 2022 with a donation by Julie on behalf of the Larsons that was matched by Adelphi. This prestigious award is a partial scholarship provided to two theater students annually over their four years at the university, and like the Jonathan Larson Grant, it too will operate in perpetuity.

The Larsons also found a way to connect the many *Rent* companies and casts to Jonathan by continuing a tradition that he and his friends had been celebrating since the eighties. It was called the Peasant's Feast and had begun as a very informal, very festive bohemian celebration for all of Jonathan's friends who couldn't afford to travel to, or for whatever reason couldn't be with, their families over Christmas. The feast was a BYOB, BYOF, BYOD soiree and had been initiated by Jonathan and his college roommate Todd Robinson at Adelphi, and it continued through the eighties into the nineties at Jonathan's apartment in the West Village. There was an ever-growing, ever-evolving rotation of regulars and new friends every year through the end of 1994. Jonathan hosted his final feast before we began rehearsals at the end of 1995, and the guest list was the newly formed *Rent* cast.

While the show was in its most frenzied global period from 1996 until 2008, the Larsons continued, whenever possible, to host Peasant's Feasts (a couple of them even occurred at the Life Café, the real-life East Village restaurant depicted in "La Vie Boheme"). For the Larson family, everything they did after Jonathan was gone was about improving lives and changing outcomes.

My mom died on October 6, 1999, thirteen months after her cancer diagnosis and way too many years ahead of her time. We buried her in a new section of the Adath Yeshurun cemetery in Minneapolis. It was very peaceful, with a large oak tree keeping watch over the area, and a creek running behind it. In a uniquely Minnesotan way, our neighbors, who were attending the funeral, loved the new area and started looking for their own burial plots before the service began. "Oh, I like this spot, Bobby," they said to my dad. "Where are you going to be? We want to be next to you and Judie." The burial plot shopping became darkly lighthearted—they were shopping for grave sites at the cemetery like they were shopping for walleye at the fishmonger. It was very Coen brothers–like (who, incidentally, grew up in the same Minneapolis suburb that we did). After the service everyone made a reservation to ensure that, eventually, that small portion of the cemetery would resemble the cul-de-sac in which I'd grown up.

The setting and the day were as idyllic as anyone would want for a funeral. The weather gods were smiling down on my mom. Unexpectedly balmy temperatures had taken over the region for a week or so and reprised an all-too-brief summer gone by. Even though we Minnesotans understand the fickleness of autumn (snow in early October isn't uncommon), we honor and respect nature and how it treats us each year, with our much-beloved four extreme seasons. Something for everyone. Hot but beautiful summers spent on the lakes. Transitional fall, stunning in its colors. Snowy winters with temperatures frequently well below zero. And the agonizingly long snowmelt through the spring months, sometimes into early May.

At the funeral my mind wandered back to my childhood. Winter of 1974. I was fifteen years old. I'd begin my days at 5:30

a.m., delivering newspapers in the early morning when it was still dark, then come home, get a nice sugar high from breakfast cereals and treats, and then get trudging, lugging my tenor sax to the bus stop, my hair and eyebrows frozen and causing me to look five times my age until the ice melted in the heated school bus. When I met my school buds at the bus stop during the winter, we all looked like senior citizens with gray, frosty eyebrows.

"*Yitgadal, v'yitkadash sh'meih raba, b'alma di v'ra chirutei.*" I snapped back to the present. Everyone was reciting the Mourner's Kaddish, the Jewish prayer for the dead. The Kaddish is spoken at services every week at synagogues and at every funeral. The Kaddish is so embedded in the culture, even the less pious reformed Jews know it. After the brief graveside service, everyone took a shovelful of dirt and dropped it on top of the pine box that housed my late mother's earthly body. The night before her death, she had asked me to get her out of bed so my dad and I could change the sheets. Prior to that she hadn't left that bed in over three months. My dad and I took care of business, and the next morning when I went to my mom to get her Caribou Coffee order (it had been the same every day, the High Rise Cooler), there was no person there, just an empty machine with a heartbeat, waiting for the quarters to run out. I knew at that moment that her soul had left her body and the planet. The previous night her soul was there, and in the morning it was gone. That was all the proof I needed. The soul animates the body.

It was in the later years of my dad's life that I learned so much about my parents and their relationship to music. They had a limited record and cassette collection, with some jazz (Duke Ellington, Ella Fitzgerald, and Dave Frishberg, who was from St. Paul), some musical theater (*Stop the World—I Want to Get Off, The Sound of Music,* and *Fiddler on the Roof*), and a little sixties pop (Burt Bacharach, Herb Alpert & The Tijuana Brass, and Bob Dylan—because my folks had known Dylan's mom since his name was Bobby Zimmerman) barely filling a shelf and a small drawer. But what they loved to do most was to go hear live music, particularly jazz singers and cabaret shows. A couple years before the iconic Dinah Washington's death in the early 1960s, they heard her at a local supper club on a typically frigid Minnesota January night. They were there for drinks, dinner, and more drinks, and following three sets of Dinah my parents were the last holdouts in the empty club. Ms. Washington came to their table after the gig and asked my dad if he knew a place where a girl could get a drink. My dad said, "Well, I sure do," and they drove her to a downtown after-hours club that my dad insured. He introduced Dinah to the club owner and politely declined the offer of a drink because they had to get home to their three young sons.

My mother was a serious pianist for a hot minute. In my oldest remembrances, I can still hear her in moments of frustration go to the piano and bang out the first four measures of the "Warsaw Concerto," part of a film score by the British composer Richard Addinsell. When I started to "play" at three years old, she mostly stopped playing. I always thought she knew then that our piano would be in use going forward, no matter what my future held.

In the months and years after my mom passed, I began to spend real quality time with my dad. He and his side of the family were completely tone-deaf, and yet his favorite "artistic" thing to do was to go hear the Minnesota Orchestra with my mom. At first I assumed he'd done it for her, but when I asked him if he'd liked it or was he just making mom happy, he said, "Yeah, I loved it."

"Why?" I asked.

"Because it made me feel good." As I came to learn, he felt that way about country and hillbilly music, which he listened to religiously every Saturday morning on Minnesota Public Radio. While I was deep into my professional career, always struggling to find the right balance between an emotional response and my habitual deconstruction of music in real time, my tone-deaf father reminded me, in his own way, of the emotionally transformative power of music. All perfectly summed up simply and beautifully. "It made me feel good."

In the summer of 2001, Michael and I began rehearsals with our first all nonunion company. Those producers had a network (the company's name was NETworks) of local promoters in many second-tier cities and college towns that could be used to get deep into the fabric of US audiences (particularly the college-aged ones Jonathan wanted his show to connect with) in a way we couldn't by exclusively playing the major markets. One of the natural outgrowths of that was some protests in the rural Midwest and below the Mason Dixon line. I loved that. It was art that moved people to protest, which was, I thought, one of its great effects on society. You either love it, hate it, or fall somewhere in between, but good art evokes an emotional, sociopolitical reaction one way or the other. We didn't get those kinds of protests in the northern, coastal, or blue-state cities, but it was a feature of some of our nonunion touring stops. Even interviews I did with a lot of the local media (mostly radio stations and newspapers) wanted to find out where I sat on the political spectrum. But for me, the conversation always needed to be centered on the show and its message: live each day to its fullest, no matter the circumstances you find yourself in. "Forget regret, or life is yours to miss," as Jonathan wrote.

One September day I decided that rather than take the subway down to Forty-Second Street for work, I would walk from my apartment on the Upper West Side. It was a perfect day, and on the way downtown I stopped for a banana at a deli near Columbus Circle, where I saw a newscast on TV about a plane that had hit the World Trade Center. The reporter said it was an accident. By the time I reached Forty-Seventh Street, masses of people were staring up at the jumbotron overlooking Times Square.

The second tower had been hit and now the newspeople were talking about the terrorist attack in New York City. In the studio on Forty-Second Street, some of the young actors were completely panicked. As it turned out, a handful of them were from in and around Washington, DC, and a few of them had parents who worked at the Pentagon, where the third plane had hit shortly after 9:30 that morning. They were frantically trying to reach their moms and dads. For many of them, the joy of their first professional job collided with the tragedy of 9/11. Thankfully all our DC kids tracked down their families and none of them lost anyone that morning, but we would exit rehearsal to find our city forever changed.

Due to 9/11, rehearsing in New York City became next to impossible, so we traveled to Charleston, South Carolina, ahead of schedule to finish rehearsals and tech, and then open our tour there. One day in Charleston there was a knock on the backstage door of our theater, and when our stage manager opened it, she was met by two FBI agents. They were looking for Richard Friedman, our sound engineer. Richard had been on the road for a long time—years in fact—and while traveling with a variety of shows, he had been taking flying lessons to get his pilot's license. That put Richard on "the list." Fortunately the FBI seemed satisfied with what Richard told them, and with our producers vouching for him, they left.

In the late fall of 2001, our Broadway show was doing fine, albeit with the necessary replacements that I was helping put into it. I was playing as often as I could, feeling very much involved with the band and like I was part of the full-time running of the show again. It was so joyful to be back in that chair. I loved playing the show; there I was, back where I belonged. We had a great second cast in there. Norbert Leo Butz, who was playing Roger, was singing and playing guitar at a party when he was discovered by Bernie; it was just after he had hit New York from Alabama, and he sounded like Sting. Wilson Cruz, who was playing Angel, had come to fame in the TV show *My So-Called Life,* and had joined the Broadway show after being in the Benny company. The cast also included Michael McElroy as Collins, Jim Poulos as Mark, Marcy Harriell as Mimi, Sherie Rene Scott as Maureen, and our beloved Gwen Stewart, who was playing Joanne. For the most part, it was as solid a second or third group as any musical director could have hoped for with many really great artists giving their best every night.

Unfortunately this wasn't true for everyone. We had fifteen onstage for much of the musical, and the success of the performance required the maximum effort of all fifteen. The energy—physical, emotional, and vocal—was starting to fray around the edges of our show. And since I believed everyone had an important role to play, we were only as good as our weakest link, and those weaker links were starting to increase in number, depending on who was performing that afternoon or evening. More people were calling out sick (or just calling out) with greater regularity, and this created more opportunities for the understudies and offstage covers, who would go on more frequently and get the valued performance reps, not to mention the increase in pay. To be honest, from where I was sitting, I didn't think some of the cast members and understudies were making the most of this opportunity. They simply didn't seem to be trying all that hard.

All the things that were happening at our show were, to a degree, typical of a lot of shows—a "sickness" known as long-run-itis. Except that we weren't a lot of shows. We were *Rent*, dammit. We weren't going to fall into those lazy habits and those minefields of ineptitude that sprung up in other musicals. Not as long as I was there. Even though I was busy with the touring of the show, and therefore less of a presence around the Nederlander, that didn't make it any less important to me. I still loved *Rent*. I loved playing *Rent*. I loved setting up, rehearsing, and mounting either sit-down productions in other countries, or the three national tours that were out, just as I loved the Broadway show. As the lyric said, "Everything is rent!" That was my life. In the space of just five years I had helped mount the Broadway company; two national touring companies; the West End company in London; the Canadian, Japanese, German, and Mexico City companies; and our first nonunion national tour. The Australian company began in late 1998, and although I took the first casting trip to Oz, I passed it along to another music supervisor to mount. That was my most sane decision during that insane run of work. Going back and forth to Australia multiple times would have been a bridge too far. If I had just done auditions and found the right musical directors for each production, my life would have been a lot less hectic, but because Michael and I had agreed early on that each show would be custom-fit to each cast, I felt I needed to be there for creative reasons and be the musical arbiter of what I thought was appropriate taste.

As egotistical as it sounds that I was the only one who could do the job, it was rooted in my seven years with the show since I began downtown in 1994. As the music supervisor, I was involved from the beginning to the end of each production: Auditions, callbacks, and casting, to finding musical directors, whether from New York or whichever country we'd be playing, to auditioning bands where necessary, ordering all the band gear, programming the newer models of keyboards and drum machines, and making sure we were printing enough scores to be sent in advance for the productions prior to rehearsal. Then integrating the musical directors into the production, through meetings, then weeks of rehearsal, first with the cast, then offsite with the band. The long hours of tech, then finally, the opening and run of each production. While the production was running, my supervisory work included trips to see the shows wherever they were playing every six weeks—more often if we were putting new people into the

MAKING RENT

show. That work continued through the run of each production.

After every show had been put up, I'd go back to be with the Broadway company. Dan Weiss was my associate musical director, but he, by his own admission, was new to the job and was still learning what to listen for and prioritize. I didn't help him very much, and you don't completely learn that skillset in a day, a week, a month, or beyond. And truthfully, I believed that I alone was the best communicator of how to execute Jonathan's music. That belief was deeply personal. So when I did get back to Broadway and saw and heard people not having as much pride in what they were doing as I thought they should have, I would become increasingly incensed.

Even though Jonathan and I had only known each other for about eighteen months, I felt I'd had an intense, meaningful relationship with him. I kept harkening back to the day he had exclaimed joyously, "I've found my collaborator!" Jonathan was a straight shooter, unapologetic about who he was and pure in his intentions. There was no trickery, manipulation, or duplicity about him, so when he said that, he meant it. I thought about that proclamation a lot over the years as I continued to mourn his loss—often even more than that of my own mother. That made obvious sense to me because I was reminded of him every night on Broadway or wherever other productions would take me, and I talked about him to everyone who would listen, whether it was during music rehearsals or at the bar after a show, like with Pop. It was therapeutic for me as well, and sharing stories about him was a way for me to dispel the grief that I still carried around.

In my profession, the relationship between a composer and a musical director is noteworthy, almost holy, because it means you share similar tastes, aesthetics, goals, and, most importantly, complete trust in one another. For the composer the trust is that the musical director will do everything to respect and elevate their work, and to keep any discussion about the work open, honest, and forthright. For the musical director the trust is that the composer will be a reliable partner, won't throw them under the bus, and won't begrudge them if the show isn't a success. Instead, the collaboration will continue and both parties will live to fight another day together. For either party, walking away from the partnership would be easy. For one thing, musical directors need to make a living, and maybe the composer needs a change, reset, or different musical voice in their ear. The reason for change could be anything, but the reasons to stay together, push forward together, continue trusting and relying on each other are personal: a shared vision, a shared dream, and an undying trust in the bond.

Not all composers want collaborators, but Jonathan knew he wanted one. We had even begun conversations about the next show we would do together, and in my mind there would be multiple collaborations. The longer he was gone, the more I felt the loss of that future for us, what he might have written, and to what heights that original, dynamic composer's voice of his would have ascended. I could see us working together scoring one of his friends' films, maybe one from Todd Robinson or Jonathan Burkhart. Maybe we'd do a record or two. Or maybe I would be a trustworthy ear and an arranger he could rely upon—a couple of like-minded musical souls sharing ideas, just as our relationship had begun.

For a few years after Jonathan's death, I was still burying a kind of unholy part of myself. Coming to grips with the truth of what I was feeling was disturbing at best and sickening at worst. The stone-cold truth was that as heartbroken as I was about his death, for a brief time I was also pissed off at Jonathan for dying just as we were getting started. That wasn't the way it was supposed to go. We were supposed to be on our professional odyssey together. This wasn't the way my professional life was supposed to turn out. I was supposed to be an integral part of a two-man wrecking crew, not "stuck" doing one show. Even if the one show

MAKING RENT
(229)

was *Rent*, the best theater gig anywhere.

My thinking, while selfish and frankly unattractive, probably wasn't limited to me alone. I thought that, for sure, his friends were pissed off that he'd died, but for them the reasons were entirely personal. There may have been projects that they would have done together, but not a shred of their grief was career-related. Matt O'Grady, Jonathan's childhood friend, framed Jonathan's passing in a way that struck a chord in me. Speaking of his death in the context of his impact on Marfan syndrome and saving countless lives, Matt said, "Jonathan died so others could live." What he said had almost a religious feel to it. After Matt shared that with me, I realized that I wasn't truly angry at Jonathan for dying. How could I be? Sure, I had overwhelming regret that what we could have created together would never come to fruition, but I didn't think my career would stall out because of his passing. If anything, I felt my success with *Rent* would ultimately lead to other Broadway shows. What Matt helped me do with his incredibly simple yet perceptive insight was crack open a part of me that was key in discovering where my real anger was coming from.

I had begun to feel a slow, relentless burn deep in my chest as we moved through our third Broadway company and prepared for our fourth. There was always some overlap, but by the fall of 2002 our cast certainly looked different from the ones in 1999, 2000, and 2001. I was little more than a mirage at the theater by then but still managed to play my required minimum number of shows and have the occasional music rehearsal when I felt it necessary. Even though we still had some great performers giving great performances from night to night, we had become, as a whole, worse. The people who knew, *knew*. Everyone heard it when they were all onstage together, especially during the large group numbers. And mostly it was due to a lack of effort, plain and simple. If someone wasn't the greatest actor or singer, I could live with that. But not giving your best? That didn't compute for me. What I wanted to say to them was, "Imagine if I came in, sat down in the chair, and thought, *I don't really feel up to playing all the notes tonight, and I don't feel like giving all the cues to the band.*" This entitlement thing was new to me. I couldn't believe that someone would think it was optional to give or not give their level best every show, and that just by virtue of being in *Rent* afforded them the privilege to do as much as they wanted, when they wanted. I mean, are you kidding me? And it was happening somewhere on that stage every night. There were some folks I wanted to ask, "Why are you so lazy in the way you approach your work? Is it because you didn't get the role you think you deserved? You're in a hit show on Broadway. Doesn't that deserve your best effort?"

Michael and I knew, going all the way back to the Angel company, that he and I weren't anywhere close to being loved, or even liked, by some of the cast. I was hurt by that reaction initially, but I got over it. What I was feeling now was the ones who cared less were hurting their fellow castmates. *That* was the height of selfishness, but maybe this was the new normal and the provincial days of always giving your best were in the rearview. It was so ingrained in me that being a professional was a meritocracy—that if you used every day, every gig, as an opportunity to improve, then one gig would naturally lead to the next better gig, and the next, and so on. But apparently I had fallen asleep for quite a while because those quaint notions now seemed obsolete. The idea of leaving the theater after the show and feeling fulfilled and proud that you did your best was old news, and I was witnessing that every night. But I pressed on, because that's what someone in my position does. I gave notes. The same ones over and over, but always from a positive viewpoint. "We need you to sing out more here because . . ." or "You need to be heard here so the group will sound more balanced." I never said, "Don't do this because. . ." but rather, "Try this, and here's why I'm asking." And still, I couldn't reach all of them. I graduated from smoldering inside to churning and burning.

There were concrete ways that I'd be able to suss out the effort being put forward. Sometimes I would sit out and watch the show from different locations in the theater, but I usually sat with the show's board operator behind the front-of-house mixing console. It was there where I could literally *see* what kind of vocal effort the actors were bringing to a performance. Each singer was assigned to a channel on the console so the board operator could mix the show in real time. If a singer was coming back from being sick, the board op could help them by nudging the slider (called a fader) up a tic or two. But those were the exceptions, not the rule. There was a baseline of vocal output that every new cast member would "set" at their own sound check before they were put into the show. My expectation was that that level, the level *they* had set, would be consistent every show. When I knew the show was sounding different, I could slip on a pair of headphones that were plugged into the console and isolate any singer at any time, just to spot-check how they were singing. Not only could I hear them, but I could also see their output, indicated by a column of red LED lights on each channel. The louder they sang, the higher the column of lights would go. On some occasions when a cast member was supposed to be singing, I would hear nothing in the headphones nor see any of the LEDs lighting up. The person was lip-synching up there, just as I had thought when I was playing the show. I could tell. Any musical director worth their salt could tell. All that amateur performing stressed me out further, if that was even possible by then. And the worst part was that I was taking that stress and anger home with me. I was no longer able to leave the show at the theater. I woke up with it, had lunch with it, and took the subway to the gig with it.

I had always thought of myself as a pretty sanguine person.

That was how I went through my adult life, the ups and downs, personally and professionally, while constantly negotiating the inconvenient realities of living in New York, whether overcrowded subway cars with no AC in the underground summer swelter, or the buckled cement I tripped over on the sidewalk. The longer I lived in Manhattan, the tighter I held on to my upper-midwestern background and values to cope, and my optimism was central to it all. Now, however, that sunshine was being eclipsed as I anticipated going to play the show every night, knowing that errors would be made, performances would be lackadaisical, and I was irritated even before I stepped into the theater. I was still me on the outside, but inside I was resentful and hostile, just waiting for a shoe to drop, a missed vocal entrance, a note not held long enough, or the now-too-common lazy diction. Each week, each show, even each act was passing in dog years. I was very aware of those feelings, but I buried them because I loved the show. I held on to it for dear life and at the same time I wanted to run away from it like an abusive girlfriend. Both things could be, and were, true. The show and I were in a toxic relationship. Still, I listened faithfully from both my place onstage and out front.

 I called music rehearsals not regularly, but responsibly. By that I mean I didn't want to browbeat them, because inevitably my words would fall on deaf ears. But since I had been compiling the same notes night after night, week after week, I began referring to them as my grocery list. Each note would be like a food staple: Bread, juice, coffee, eggs. "Hold this note longer, better diction, and the word is pronounced '*Kuro*sawa,' like Coors beer." When a musical director gives notes the expectation is that, even if you have to give them more than once, there will be a concerted effort by the actors to implement them. Accumulating my grocery list over multiple weeks told me that impulse to correct and improve wasn't anywhere in the vicinity of our theater. As a matter of fact, I concluded, they gave them no thought or consideration whatsoever.

My music rehearsals were usually on Thursdays, due to our weekly schedule. One particular Thursday rehearsal, sometime in the fall of 2002 (I don't remember the exact date because my *Rent* life was still a blur), began like any other, with the cast sitting on the tables and chairs that we used in the show, facing me while I sat at the keyboard. I always liked to start by giving my general feeling about the musical state of the show. I told them how I had sat out at the board the previous weekend and how disappointed I was to hear or not hear, see or not see, evidence of some of them barely, or not, making a sound while they were supposed to be singing. *Again.* Then, rather than trying to patiently urge them, *again,* to be better, I went from zero to a hundred in a split second.

"I CAN'T FUCKING BELIEVE YOU'RE NOT SINGING WHEN YOU'RE FACING UPSTAGE! JUST BECAUSE THE AUDIENCE CAN'T SEE YOU IS NO EXCUSE TO JUST STOP FUCKING SINGING! AND FOR THOSE OF YOU WHO ARE JUST LIP-SYNCHING, I KNOW IT BECAUSE I CAN SEE YOUR BODY NOT FUCKING BREATHING! WHAT, YOU DON'T THINK I CAN'T FUCKING SEE THAT? WHAT DO YOU THINK I AM, FUCKING STUPID? WHAT THE FUCK IS WRONG WITH YOU? YOU'RE UP THERE STEALING MONEY AND YOU'RE DISRESPECTING THE SHOW! DON'T YOU FUCKING GET IT? I MEAN, THE COMPOSER LITERALLY FUCKING GAVE HIS LIFE SO YOU COULD BE UP HERE! IF THAT DOESN'T MEAN ANYTHING TO YOU, THEN YOU'RE JUST A SELFISH PRICK AND AS FAR AS I'M CONCERNED YOU SHOULD FUCKING LEAVE THE SHOW. NOW! REALLY, I'M NOT KIDDING! GET THE FUCK OUTTA HERE!"

I had a straight-up meltdown. Rather than getting notes as they always had, what the cast got from me instead was the worst version of my humanity. Ever. I was half screaming and half crying when I laid down that stirring, inspirational, uplifting diatribe from the chair next to my keyboard setup in Crazytown. The fact that they weren't performing to the best of their ability was unprofessional, and that was *their* problem. What wasn't their problem was my grief journey or the fact that this couldn't ever be the same show we'd built at the Workshop and moved to Broadway, a show dedicated to Jonathan's memory in the most full-hearted ways imaginable. The original cast and creative team had lived through an experience that had never happened before and hopefully would never happen again. This new group hadn't lived it. And my unfair, unreal expectation of them, that their dedication to the show should be as emotionally packed as mine, was *my* problem. I wanted the Broadway show to be just like the one from six years ago, and I knew in my soul I was asking the impossible.

It got worse. Instead of that episode being an emotional cleansing for me, I continued to take my resentment out on them internally, toting my own emotional Seven Dwarfs with me to the Nederlander every night—Cranky, Moody, Pissy, Crotchety, Grumpy, Testy, and Irascible. I was completely shredded, and the company was now, once and for all, over me and my irritable charmlessness. I knew what I had to own. In addition to what felt like a lifetime of work compressed into almost seven years, and the heartbreak that threw everything into a harrowing overdrive that I still hadn't shaken, I was still haunted by Jonathan's death, the loss of my mother, the stress of a failed marriage, and even the stresses of my recent one to Randy (we'd been married for a few years by then). I kept my feelings buried beneath my unending responsibility to *Rent,* still rooted in my own need to maintain the promises and commitments to Jonathan, his friends, and his family that I had privately sworn to uphold. And yet, I was hoping that somehow, some way, everything would sort itself out and that at a certain point I would be able to calmly and rationally compartmentalize the two most important things in my life: the show, which I knew was the best thing ever to happen to me

MAKING RENT

professionally, and Randy, who I knew was the best thing to ever happen to me personally.

After yelling at a company that didn't deserve to be yelled at, it had become abundantly clear that I needed to remove myself from a situation that was only going downhill. I finally allowed myself the sad realization that the production I had helped raise from its downtown infancy and helped shepherd to Broadway was the one I had to let go of. It was best for everyone, but mostly for me. I was spent. I had turned sour, rancid, and unpleasant—in other words, I was long past my expiration date. I gave management my notice and left the Broadway company. There was no celebration, no goodbyes, no party, not even a toast over a cocktail. One day I was there and the next day I wasn't. Simple as that.

I mostly stayed away from the Broadway production for the next six years, until the show closed, only showing up perfunctorily to check in on it. My job, when I wasn't the musical director, defaulted to the same job I had with all the other companies, music supervisor. It was very nice that our producers and general manager never put any undue pressure on me to go check in on the Broadway show more often than I wanted. I was fine to go visit our nonunion tour, which was doing well, and going to see the last vestiges of our other North American tours until they ran their courses and shut down.

Over the ensuing years I got involved in quite a few other projects, and I was grateful to find a professional life after *Rent*. I kept the show close to me by way of my fellow *Rent* bandmates, whom I dragged around to every gig I did. This began in the summer of 2002 with the original motion picture soundtrack to the cult classic film *Camp*, directed by Todd Graff (who is Randy's cousin). I did all the musical direction and arrangements for the film, and the soundtrack included the *Rent* stalwarts: me on piano and synthesizer, Kenny on guitars and banjo, Dan playing organ and guitar, Jeff on drums, and Tony Conniff, one of our earliest bass subs, on bass. All those guys got plenty of screen time in the "live" music sequences of the movie—so if you've seen the film, there they are: the *Rent* band, live and in living color.

In 2006 it was my honor to produce and arrange the concert for Jonathan's enshrinement into the Library of Congress, where all his work was curated into the library's permanent archives. The original *Rent* band, all five of us, were there to play and celebrate the occasion. In 2007 I was the musical director for the Patty Griffin musical *10 Million Miles*, at the Atlantic Theater Company, with Dan on acoustic and electric guitar, Tony on bass, and our first-ever *Rent* sub, Bobby Baxmeyer, on guitars and mandolin. Bobby Bax, as I called him, was a multi-instrumentalist, and he stayed with the show for many years, playing both the lead guitar chair and the guitar/keyboard chair on Broadway and on multiple tours. Since he was the first sub in the history of the *Rent* band, they bestowed on him the title the "fifth Beatle."

In 2008 I was the musical director and conductor of Jeanine Tesori's *Shrek the Musical*, and sure enough there were Kenny and Bobby Bax again, holding down the two guitar chairs. That rhythm section was so awesome that I dubbed them the "Shrekking Crew," an homage to the Wrecking Crew, the incredible cast of Los Angeles session players who had recorded hundreds of hit records during the 1960s and 1970s. In 2015 I would do my last Broadway show, *Lady Day at Emerson's Bar & Grill*, starring Audra McDonald and directed by Lonny Price. Yes, the same Lonny on whose couch I'd slept, who had told me to never leave *Rent* and who had fixed me up with Randy. *That's* friendship. The drummer in the *Lady Day* trio was Clayton Craddock, who had subbed for Jeff in *Rent* fifteen years prior.

In between *Shrek* and *Lady Day* I was asked to do *Rent* at the Hollywood Bowl, with the show to be directed by Neil Patrick Harris, and we put up the show in record time with a cast about double the size it was for the Broadway production. The show was star-studded, with recognizable actors across television, film, and music: Skylar Astin (Mark), Wayne Brady (Collins), Vanessa Hudgens (Mimi), Telly Leung (Angel), Nicole Scherzinger (Maureen), Tracie Thoms (Joanne), Aaron Tveit (Roger), and Collins Pennie (Benny). The paparazzi was already staking out the parking lot where everyone showed up to go to work by day two of rehearsal. It didn't take long for a security detail to arrive, and the actors didn't seem the least bit bothered. They were all used to it, I guessed. We expanded the band as well, from the original five-piece rhythm section to a twelve-piece orchestra, adding strings, reeds, brass, and percussion. Three of us from the original *Rent* band were on the gig—Kenny, Dan, and me, plus two of the heavyweights from our Benny company band, Simeon Pillich on bass and Alan Childs on drums. We had made it from our humble beginnings at NYTW to the legendary Hollywood Bowl. Even though Jeff wasn't on that gig, I could still hear him saying, "Look what's happened to our little show."

I suffered a massive heart attack two weeks after the Hollywood Bowl. I was on the operating table, completely drugged up for a quadruple bypass, when I went into full-on cardiac arrest and had a stroke. When I got to my hospital bed hours later, the first flowers I saw were from Neil Patrick Harris. Even though I wasn't fully conscious for about a week, those flowers made me the closest thing to a celebrity on my hospital floor. I never thanked Neil for that. Thank you, Neil. My recovery was long and sometimes arduous, and I had so much metal in my chest, it looked like a construction site in Midtown Manhattan.

After I returned to New York in early 2011, I did the first reading of *Motown: The Musical*. It was great to meet the legendary Berry Gordy, but my stamina and patience weren't up to the task. I went to London and helped as best I could with the West End production of *Shrek,* but I had to fly back early because my heart health still needed more attention. The next year or so was dotted with trips back to Englewood Hospital in New Jersey to get additional stents and some of my originals replaced. By early 2012 I was fully recovered, and I helped put up an off-Broadway production of *Rent* at New World Stages on West Fiftieth Street.

During the eighteen or so months of my recovery I had time to reflect on all that Jonathan had done beyond *Rent* for American musical theater. He had done what he'd told everyone he'd do: he changed the sound of many musicals, making it cool to have rock, pop, R & B, Latin, and even rap ("Today 4 U") as the musical backdrop to the storytelling audiences experienced. That rhythm-section-forward approach manifested itself in so many shows, beginning with *Hedwig and the Angry Inch,* which opened in 1997, to *American Idiot* in 2010. In between were shows like *Rock of Ages, Spring Awakening, Passing Strange, Next to Normal, In the Heights,* and *Memphis,* to name a handful (still to come would be the next once-in-a-generation musical, *Hamilton*). The writers of most of those shows, and those that came after them, were clearly standing on the shoulders of Jonathan Larson.

Another sea change he helped bring about was the style of singing that now routinely populates many Broadway shows. Unlike in the old days, when Bernie, Will, and David had to scrape and scramble to find singers who understood contemporary music as well as the traditional musical theater repertoire, those voices are now everywhere. Just the actors who have played Maureen over the years—Idina, Eden Espinosa, Sherie Rene Scott, to name a few—have had enormous success, to say nothing of the many other men and women from our show, including Adam Pascal, Anthony Rapp, Norbert Leo Butz, Leslie Odom Jr., Robin de Jesús, Jeremy Kushnier, Will Chase, Renée Elise Goldsberry, Kenna Ramsey, Merle Dandridge, and Daphne Rubin-Vega, whose Mimi opened doors for many women of Latin ancestry in the industry and helped usher in generations of contemporary Latin singers on Broadway.

And lastly there were all the careers Jonathan either helped launch or send further into the stratosphere. From the New York Theatre Workshop itself to Michael and me; Adam, Anthony, Taye, Jesse, Daphne, and Idina; and Bernie, Will, and David, just to name a tiny few of us. That list is seemingly endless, and so it is with my own gratitude.

Beyond writing a few more musicals, it's pure speculation as to what path Jonathan's career might have taken, but this I know for sure: in the short time I knew him, I learned that he was an innovator, a serial boundary pusher, and an adventurous creative spirit. The possibilities would have been endless.

In 2015 the most unexpected and welcome call came from my dear friend Evan Ensign, a veteran Broadway stage manager and a fine director who had been the associate director on *Rent* for more than ten years. He and I would put up *Rent*'s twentieth anniversary tour, the first of five *Rent* tours with Work Light Productions. Evan and I had done four nonunion tours with NETworks back in the early 2000s, so this was nothing new for us except that in the ensuing years *Rent* had become a period piece, a sociocultural historical marker of an earlier time. As a result, Evan's first job was to bring the cast back to the time of the HIV/AIDS crisis in America. That landscape had changed significantly since the mid-1990s, due primarily to HAART, the acronym for highly active antiretroviral therapy, or as it was often called, "the cocktail." Overall new HIV infections in America decreased by 73 percent between the peak of the crisis in 1983–1984 and 2019.

Since we didn't have the luxury of a lengthy rehearsal time frame, Evan used the 2003 VH1 documentary *AIDS: A Pop Culture History* as a gateway and crash course for our new generation of millennials and Gen Zers to learn about how the AIDS crisis tore the world apart. For our cast members, many of whom didn't know anyone who had HIV, let alone anyone who had died from AIDS, learning the stories about familiar pop culture icons like Freddie Mercury, Magic Johnson, Rock Hudson, Eazy-E, and Arthur Ashe helped put the crisis into a more accessible context. If those people had died from AIDS, then it wasn't a reach to understand how deeply HIV/AIDS had burrowed itself into society and that the *Rent* characters they would inhabit would be affected by that in multiple ways. When they learned, early in the musical, that Angel, Collins, Roger, and his late girlfriend all had AIDS, they immediately understood the life-and-death stakes that informed the weighty backbone of the show. That was when I understood why Evan had chosen a video so relatable to our casts. They could see themselves in those celebrities. No matter who they were, the people in that documentary were all part of the sickness, death, rebellion, and activism that became central to those of us who lived through that period in American life. Between the backdrop of HIV/AIDS and their own experiences as young artists vying to be seen and heard in contemporary society, our casts embraced *Rent*'s values of community and lasting friendship. Those values felt brand-new in every production we mounted, no matter how many times Evan and I had been through it, because the young artists who inhabited those roles were unique and the sum of the community they formed was equally distinct.

I came into those first rehearsals with our producers, Steve and Nancy Gabriel, our cast, and our management team with a renewed sense of purpose. I was still feeling all the positivity of my life having been saved by trying to live a healthier lifestyle, and I was grateful for my second chance. I even had a new lease on *Rent*. At last I was unencumbered by my sadness, anger, and bitterness from thirteen years prior (note to self: no f-bomb–laced tirades aimed at this young, wonderful cast) and was able, once again, to fully appreciate my time with the show I loved so much.

I was downright giddy at the prospect of helping this new generation of artists reap the benefits of Jonathan's beautiful, life-affirming masterpiece.

As I had in 1994, the first time I began *Rent* music rehearsals with "Seasons of Love," I led the cast in a vocal warmup (including the Stevie Wonder exercises), and then I said to them what I'd said to so many casts over so many years:

"Okay, everyone, you ready? Let's carve."

Pop and me in London, 1998.

OUTRO

IN SEPTEMBER 2016, I was sitting in the theater on the campus of Indiana University in Bloomington, Indiana. Al Larson was with me. Even at ninety-one, Pop still wanted to come out and meet the new casts that would be performing *Rent*, and this was the night of the new tour's first preview. Pop and I had arrived early and all of us stood in a circle on the stage before the audience came in, holding hands and singing "Seasons of Love," another *Rent* tradition since its beginnings. Everyone always crowded around Pop after the singing was over, and it made him feel like a part of the show. For our casts, being with Pop was as direct a connection to Jonathan as they could get.

We took our seats on the aisle, and as the audience was filing in, a man, probably in his mid- to late forties, just happened to look down and see me with my *Rent* credential hanging around my neck. He took a second look at me, noticed the notepad in my hand, and asked, "Are you with the show?" I told him I was. Then he said, "I know this might sound weird, but you look familiar. Were you ever in the show?" I told him I was the conductor on Broadway, and he exclaimed, "I knew I recognized you!" He introduced me to his son, who looked like he was about thirteen.

"This is the first time he's seen *Rent* onstage," he said. "He's seen the movie, but I told him seeing the show live is totally different and that's why we're here, so he can experience what I saw on Broadway in the nineties."

We exchanged introductions and then I introduced them to Pop. "This is Al Larson," I said. "He's the father of Jonathan Larson, who wrote the show." The father excitedly shook his hand, and as usual Pop was gracious and a little shy. As they were leaving to find their seats the father said to him, "It was such an honor to meet you." I was used to that. Whether at the theater or a bar, I never tired of seeing people react to meeting Jonathan Larson's father.

After we sat back down, I said to Pop, "Did you see what just happened there, with that father bringing his kid to see the show? Your son's musical has officially jumped to the next generation. I'd bet you it won't be the last, except you won't be around to pay it off." Pop, usually with a quick retort to that kind of smart-alecky remark by me, just sat there. I swear he got a little misty-eyed. In all our years together, Pop had never *ever* visibly shown his emotions, but he gave himself away when he took out his handkerchief, wiped his glasses and dabbed his eyes. He knew.

ACKNOWLEDGMENTS

It takes a village to raise an author. Thank you to everyone who helped get this book off my computer and into literary land. The team at Apollo Publishers, especially Julia Abramoff, Victoria Black, who designed the cover and interior of the book, and my fantastic, insightful editor, Drew Anderla, whose notes, ideas, and comments were eye-opening and thought-provoking. To my very wise friends and peers who helped me along the way: Jeff Potter, writer and drummer extraordinaire, who gave me the best advice I could hope for as a first-time author. Paula Kalustian, Ted Pappas, and my long-time collaborator and best pal, Lonny Price. To all the interviewees, especially Michael Greif, Jim Nicola, and Bernie Telsey, these are your stories as well. Thanks to Jeffrey Seller, Kevin McCollum, Tori Lynn, Neil Patrick Harris, Jennifer Ashley Tepper, Mark Sendroff, Jason Aylesworth, Sherry Bloom, Steve Kennedy, Jonathan Burkhart, Victoria Leacock Hoffman, Matt O'Grady, Todd Robinson, and Janet Charleston. And to my beautiful wife, Randy Graff, who, when I'd get stuck would remind me, "Get to the feeling."

And finally to the vast *Rent* family out there: the casts, musicians, crews, management, and producers, and Jonathan's amazing family and friends. Whether or not you're name-checked in the book, you're all in it. Every last one of you.

PHOTO CREDITS

Page

ii–iii	Courtesy of Stewart Ferebee
2	Courtesy of the author
6	Courtesy of the Jonathan Larson Papers
12	Courtesy of Victoria Leacock Hoffman
16	Courtesy of the author
50	Courtesy of Anthony Rapp
82	Courtesy of Anthony Rapp
114	Courtesy of the author
122	Courtesy of Joan Marcus
135	Courtesy of the Jonathan Larson Papers
152	Courtesy of Anita Flanagan
172	Courtesy of Lyn Hughes
186	Courtesy of the Jonathan Larson Paper
198	Courtesy of the author
242	Courtesy of the author